KIDNAPPING
the POPE

A Vatican Intrigue Mystery

Leonard F. Badia and Michael F. Capobianco

Lord, make me an instrument...
—St. Francis of Assisi

Table of Contents

Chapter 1

Domenico degli Alfieri

he Roman pavement baked hot and dry that morning as the Vatican Secretary of State, Domenico degli Alfieri stared out of the window of his study completing his meditation. He was watching the cascading waters of the nearer of the square's two baroque fountains—the only hint of coolness in an otherwise scorching day.

Another Sunday, he thought, *but what a very different one it would be. None but a few handpicked men had any idea what was about to transpire on this particular Sunday.*

Even with all of his well-laid plans, Domenico degli Alfieri was to find it to be even more unusual than he anticipated.

As he tried to force himself to relax, Domenico went over it all again. Yes, everything was in order. Every conceivable factor had been meticulously accounted for, nothing would go wrong. It was vitally important that nothing go wrong!

Today, less than a decade from the turn of the century, the Church would begin to turn in a new direction. It had been long overdue. The church had long needed to turn in a direction of the future that could lead to greater acceptance of individual differences, even, Domenico mused, his own presently unacceptable preferences. Yes, it needed to be done. There had really been no choice in all of this. It was just, what they had done. It was in accordance with God's holy will. He was speaking through them so that more of the masses could be brought into the church. It must be so if the church was to survive in the new era of liberalism that was encompassing the world all around them.

Why hadn't Pope Pius XIII been able to see this as clearly as he did? He had tried on numerous occasions to speak openly with the pontiff about the obvious changes in the world around them. So many times when it seemed they were close to being of the same mindset, the pontiff would revert back to his steadfastly old fashioned, even archaic ideas of what Christendom was to be defined as. With the dawn of the modern age even the pontiff should have been able to discern the signs of the times.

Domenico leaned back in his high-backed leather chair, and was about to raise his long, thin legs to the top of his desk when the room resounded with the loud, vulgar ring of his telephone.

Domenico degli Alfieri pounced on the receiver.

"You imbecile!" he shouted. "I left orders not to be disturbed under any circumstances."

He heard his secretary's mousy voice apologetically try to defuse his master's obvious anger at being interrupted, "I am sorry, your Eminence, but it is Monsignor Maestoso. He insists on speaking to you."

"Insists, does he?" Domenico spit out with increasing anger, "Let him insist all day if he likes. I will not talk to him or anyone else! Is that clear?"

"But, your...."

Domenico slammed down the receiver vowing to replace his blatantly ineffective secretary. What good is a secretary that cannot handle unwanted visitors when he had been given such explicit orders not to disturb his master! Tomorrow he would seek to replace the imbecile.

Maestoso, of all people! He was in no mood to talk to anyone, let alone to that fat, retrograding idiot. It was wrong, he supposed, to think like that. Unchristian, of course, but as long as he could remember, he never had much use for fat people. There was no reason to be fat. It was ugly. There were jolly fat people like his father, coming as he did from Naples, probably the jolliest of cities. Much better to be muscular and wire-thin, as he himself was, the way his good German mother had always exhorted him to be.

Domenico smiled as he thought of his mother. "Look how beautifully he swims, my Domenico," she would say. He used to swim with his younger brother at a beach on the snake-like island of Procida. They lived on Capri in Anacapri, that village at the very summit of the island that was nothing more than the peak of a submerged mountain to begin with. Anacapri was always cool and quiet. Very few of the tourists went there. Most of them would get off the *funiculare* at Capri, the town at the lower level, and spend their time there in the crazy busy shops. Few would even see the best things *there*. How many, for instance, would get to the Diefenbaker gallery in the Certosa di San Giacomo? They did not know what they were missing.

8

Domenico remembered when his mother first took him there. He must have been no more than eight or nine. He never forgot the majestic impression those huge, incredibly dark paintings made on him. Even now, at fifty-two, the thought of them still thrilled him. He and his mother had appreciated the finer things of life. His fat jolly father seemed more interested in satisfying his belly than his mind. Perhaps that was his father had died at an early age. Domenico had always vowed to be more like his mother than his father, a fact that seemed interesting to him now as he considered some of the lifestyle choices he had made for himself.

"Enough of this," he said out loud to shake himself out of his reminiscing. "It is not thrills from invigorating paintings that I need now. I certainly do not need to listen to the sound of Maestoso's thick Roman voice either. No, I need to relax and calm my nerves."

He needed his strength. He had to be completely composed with the audience only a few days away. Nothing must distract him from his self-appointed mission.

"Telemann!" he said with conviction, "That is exactly what I need. That would do it."

He walked across the quietly appointed room, the cushioned carpet pleasantly yielding to his step. His record collection was small, but selective. It was kept on several shelves alongside the record player. He chose a disk, started the phonograph, and returned to his chair.

Good to have disks, he thought. *Much better than tapes as so many were using today. One cannot regard anything that can easily be erased as part of a permanent collection.*

Domenico laughed as he realized he had just chosen what some of the young people of today would consider old fashioned. However, in comparison to the stubbornness of the pontiff, he considered himself much more open minded and in tune with the current world around them. As the opening passage of the D Major Horn concerto sounded out, he quieted his thoughts and allowed his mind to relax and bask in the beauty of the music.

It was his maternal grandfather who lived with them on Capri who had first introduced him to Telemann. How strange the ways of the Lord can be at times. Here both his parents were dead, and yet his grandfather, nearly one hundred now, was still alive and vital.

"Telemann has a secret," his grandfather said the day he introduced his grandson to the music.

"Tell me what it is, Nonno," Domenico asked seeing the excitement in his beloved grandfather.

"Well, Telemann being German, knows well the power of the brass. The trumpets of judgment blend well with the triumph of the horns. But at the same time, he appreciates the Italian sweetness of the strings. It is this combination that makes this music great. Do you understand? The combination is much like you, Domenico."

Grandfather was right, of course, he *was* a combination. That very combination was what had brought him to this place of intrigue. He had tried all of the ways of "Italian sweetness," but to no avail. No, it was a time for precision, boldness, and execution if there was to be an ultimate victory against those who would hold the church back from moving into the new century.

The music was suddenly corrupted by a foreign sound invading his solitude—a short, loud hiss. It jarred Domenico's absorption, agitating him once again. Must he constantly put up with these intrepid interruptions! Looking around to discern the source of this latest interruption, he realized something was being slid under the door. He jumped up quickly and found a note on the floor.

Hurriedly, his gaunt fingers were so agitated he had difficulty unfolding the sheet of stationary.

I know your secret. You will be stopped!
Carlo Maestoso

The fool! Who does he think he is? What does he think he knows? Stopped indeed! I will see to it we are not stopped. What could he possibly know? Could he have found out even a portion of his well laid plans? Domenico had been so incredibly careful and meticulous in his dealings with the few involved that he doubted if even Carlo could have knowledge of every detail, How far back could his knowledge possibly go? Even that first day when Domenico brought the forces together, he was careful to discreetly meet when only a few of the staff were on duty.

Domenico went to his desk, Telemann still echoing throughout the room, and reached for the telephone. He would double check all the details one more time. Nothing, absolutely nothing could be allowed to intervene now. They were too close to achieving victory!

Chapter 2

The Meetings

On the day Cardinal Domenico degli Alfieri had set his plan in motion, he had trusted only his chosen messenger to escort his guests to his office. He waited in his office for Luis Ramon Conde-del-Restreppo from the Americas, and Eugeny Gregorovitch Bassarian from the Soviet Union to arrive through a well-guarded back entrance. He had called the meeting well afer normal working hours so that very few of the staff would have been aware of the meeting of the unlikely trio.

Luis Ramon Conde-del-Restreppo represented the interests of several Latin American governments. He was a robust, soiled-looking man who liked casual dress and tended to sprawl rather than sit on furniture. A stubby beard hid the lower half of his face. His left hand was often under his chin smoothing his beard, while his thumb and index finger constantly reached up to smooth out his thick moustache. He had the look of one who had just come from herding cattle on the plains. Domenico thought he could detect an odor about this man and had to consciously restrain himself from turning up his nose every time the man moved. When he spoke Italian, it sounded like Spanish. In fact, his Italian *was* a mixture of Spanish and Italian that was also very offensive to the well-educated Vatican Secretary of State.

Eugeny Gregorovitch Bassarian was an official of the Soviet government. Born of an Armenian father and a Moscovite mother, he was bilingual and had been since childhood. He had recently learned Italian and spoke it quite well Domenico thought. He was a slight man who had clearly inherited his father's Armenian features—the olive, Greek-like complexion, the dense eye-brows, and the prominent nose. His dark hair was cropped very short, and his face impeccably clean-shaven. Of the two men, Domenico was much more impressed with Bassarian.

Domenico had just introduced the two men to each other. He had spoken to each of the men individually prior to this meeting, but today they needed to be absolutely sure they were all on the same page. Domenico needed to make absolutely sure he was in full control of all facets of this operation. He was totally convinced anything less would jeopardize the entire operation.

"Well, gentlemen," he said, "from previous communications you know why we are here."

"Si," Restreppo said, "and the governments I represent would first like to know exactly with whom they are dealing. Señor Bassarian, what precisely is your title?"

The Russian laughed loudly, though to Domenico it was obvious it was not due to what the man considered humorous.

"In my line of work," Bassarian said, "we do not carry titles. Please, I am not accustomed to being addressed as 'Signore' or the like. Our practice is to call everyone 'Tavarishch' meaning 'Comrade.' Try to say it. It is a pretty word and not at all hard to say. We should all learn a little Russian, no?"

The little man was visibly shaken when Domenico shot back in rapid, flawless Russian. Pleased with the impact his interruption brought, he proved to both men he was in charge of this meeting.

"I will be happy to converse with you, Tavarishch Bassarian, in Russian anytime you wish," he added in Russian, but then continued in Italian, "But for our present purposes, we had better use a language we all know."

Domenico was, of course, also bilingual from childhood and found it enjoyable and easy to learn foreign languages. Much of the mystery of Russian disappeared, he found, upon learning the alphabet. Once one learned to pronounce words, many cognates were discovered. He also found it strange that the verb ending for the second personal plural (polite) was exactly like Italian, and so was the plural of certain nouns. This made Russian conversation seem very natural to him. The grammar was atrociously difficult, but having had to work his way through Latin and Greek (also a help in learning the Cyrillic alphabet), he managed that quite well, too.

I will play Eugeny Gregorovitch's little game, he thought, knowing he himself was in complete charge of the situation.

"Certainly, my dear Gregorovitch, we will call you Tavarishch," Domenico added in a voice that sounded slightly condescending. "I am sure you both are well aware of how to address me."

Bassarian looked a little flustered at the ease with which Domenico had turned the tables on him. Obviously the Russian was used to having the upper hand. Domenico smiled inwardly at the man's obvious loss of composure.

"Señor, Tavarisch, Your Eminence—what the hell's the difference what we call each other," said Restreppo interspersed in his uncouth manner. "Let's just get down to business."

"Yes," Domenico agreed. "Let's get down to the business at hand."

Emulating an air of dominance, Domenico leaned far back in his chair, and brought his hands together, palms facing each other almost in a gesture of prayer. However, prayer was the furthest thing from his mind at the moment. He deliberately spread his fingers apart, and let each one individually press on its opposite partner as he set the stage for the interchange that was about to occur. After a moment of poignant silence, he began a very deliberate and well-rehearsed monologue, making it perfectly clear it was not open for comment or interruption from either of his "guests."

"The governments you both represent have obviously recognized that they can no longer exclude religion from politics. It has become clear to them that trying to pretend it does not exist just does not work in today's world. They are ready now, perhaps for the first time in history, to cooperate with the Church to achieve a common goal. But it is a two-way street. Your governments cannot bring their political ideas to fruition as long as we have the present rigid and stultified leadership in the church. Neither can those of my persuasion make appropriate overtures without a more liberal administration."

Both men duly acknowledged these statements and refrained from comment knowing the Secretary of State had not yet come to the point. They both were aware of both Domenico's power and his lifestyle preferences as he put it.

"It is in this spirit, then, that I have brought you together today," Domenico said as he nodded to each man. "In a spirit of a new cooperation, and cementing of relations to the point that both our missionaries and your proselytizers can feel free to operate anywhere in the world, east or west, I am willing to take steps, with your help, to replace the present church leadership with a man with broader views. My attitude in this endeavor is that we will be acting as instruments in the carrying out of the unerring will of the Lord to move us all forward into the new century."

Unable to restrain himself any longer, Bassarian interjected, "We have the best eliminators in the world."

"What bullshit!" shouted Restreppo in quick response. "Ours may not be as subtle, but they certainly are quicker."

"Gentlemen," Domenico interjected, correcting their obvious misinterpretation, "I do not believe we will have any need of either of your brand of 'eliminators.' In fact, there are going to be certain rules regarding this operation that must be followed without deviation. Everything is to be executed according to these rules or there will not be any operation at all."

He said the last words slowly, and with very deliberate emphasis making direct eye contact with first one and then the other.

"One," he continued dramatically, "no one is to be physically harmed in any way."

"But...," the two men protested almost simultaneously.

"Two," Domenico effectively cut them off, "only certain persons will be informed of our activities. We must keep the facts concerning this operation to a very limited few."

"Three, it must be done swiftly with an absolute minimum of violence of any kind—preferably none!"

"Four, and most important, I, and only I, am in charge. Everyone will act only on *my* orders, and nothing shall take place which has not been ordered by me. I have a plan, and it is to be meticulously followed!" Domenico declared emphatically.

"So, gentlemen, or Tavarishchi, or whatever you like, if you agree, my plan will work and be of mutual benefit to all of us concerned. If you do not agree, there will be nothing accomplished and it will be as if this meeting never happened! What do you say?"

"It appears we have not much choice," said Bassarian conceded.

Restreppo looked equally convinced as he nodded and said, "We agree."

Domenico lowered his head and cast his eyes down slightly as he whispered, "Exactly!"

Knowing Dr. Enrico Lucreto, the pope's personal physician, was about to arrive and report on the pontiff's health, Domenico asked Bassarian and Restreppo to leave via the same back entrance they had come in through. He assured them he would be in touch in the near future.

"Sit down, won't you, Doctore?" Domenico invited Dr. Lucreto a few moments later, extending his right arm towards a comfortable stuffed chair.

"Grazie," Lucreto said in a squeak-like whisper, clearly uncomfortable in Domenico's presence.

Lucreto always seemed to whisper when he spoke—like a priest advising a penitent in the confessional. This manner undoubtedly developed throughout his long career as a result of his innumerable consultations with patients. He was very thorough in explaining their illnesses to them in minute detail, and this whisper-like speech created an atmosphere of intimacy and security; a grave illness seemed somehow less serious when Lucreto talked about it.

He adjusted the monocle in his right eye and sat down, his hands tightly clasped on his lap. His nervous gestures did not go unnoticed by Domenico.

"May I smoke, Your Eminence?" Lucreto asked in a tremulous whisper.

"Of course," Domenico said giving the doctor the time he needed to achieve his composure.

Lucreto took out a leather cigarette case and carefully removed a Nationale. As he brought the cigarette to his lips, Domenico produced a flame from a tiny lighter he had picked up from his desk. Lucreto jerked his head back as if afraid Domenico might burn him.

"Thank you, Your Eminence. Thank you," Lucreto said attempting to cover his obvious knee jerk reaction to Domenico coming so close to his face.

"Prego, you are welcome," Domenico said calmly as he settled back in his chair

"Tell me, then," he said looking directly into the doctor's eyes, "How is the Holy Father's health?"

"Splendid!" Lucreto said without looking at Domenico. "The man is in remarkably good health."

"I suspected as much," Domenico said as he leaned slightly forward toward the doctor, "But in your medical opinion, don't you think he is working too hard?"

"Well," Lucreto said slowly as he nervously adjusted his monocle and shifted jerkily in his chair, "I—"

"With all the stress and strain of his job, the Holy Father could surely use a change of scenery and atmosphere, don't you think?" Domenico pressed as he leaned even closer to the doctor's face.

"Well, everyone should get away from his routine once in a while," admitted the doctor seeing Domenico was finally giving him a clue as to why he had been invited to this meeting at such an odd time of the day.

"Precisely," Domenico said, sitting back in his chair as he could finally see the doctor was beginning to track with him, "and as I recall His Holiness has not had a break in a very long time now. Did you recommend the need for a short break to him?"

"Well, no. I…."

"But, my dear doctor, you do see the necessity of it, don't you?" Domenico said leaning almost threateningly toward Lucreto again.

Lucreto coughed out a puff of smoke, obviously shaken by Domenico's sudden change in position. Wanting to end this conversation and get out of there as quickly as possible, Lucreto crushed out his half cigarette with rapid, pumping motions, pressing the lighted tip against the bottom of an ash tray so hard he nearly burned the end of his finger.

"Your Eminence—ah—understand me please," Lucreto said as he made one last effort to avoid committing to something he knew he would regret later.

"Yes?" Domenico said as he pressed in, knowing there was something else on the good doctor's mind.

Domenico had become a good judge of body language and could generally tell when someone was on the verge of being "persuaded" to do something he wanted them to do. This man could be bought, he was sure of it. It was just a matter of discerning the right incentive to move Lucreto into action.

"Ah—I know, that is, I *think* I know, ah—your...," stuttered the doctor, obviously fearful of the reaction his request would invoke from the powerful man sitting in front of him.

"Merciful Lord in Heaven!" Domenico said in mock impatience. "Out with it! What are you trying to say?"

"I...I know you and the Holy Father are..." Lucreto began slowly as if feeling his way through a dark and dangerous passageway.

"You know my views regarding the pontiff," Domenico said, gesturing with his hands as if trying to hurry the frightened doctor into getting to the point, "I have not exactly kept that a secret, have I?"

"Yes...no," fumbled the doctor, "but I...."

"My dear doctor," Domenico forced himself to calm down and take his time, "I am merely asking you to suggest a vacation the pontiff take a much needed vacation—a week in the mountains for some fresh air and skiing."

"But, you see, I need...," the doctor bent his head and looked down at the floor as if expecting a physical retribution for not immediately agreeing to Domenico's suggestion.

Domenico could see it was time to place his final card, "But tell me, how is your good sister?"

Lucreto gagged, and coughed loudly surprised Domenico knew about his sister. Very few people knew he had quietly sent her away to a sanitarium far from the city. He had tried for years to treat her himself, but things had gotten to the point he could no longer conceal her often self-destructive behaviors.

"Your Eminence knows she has not been well," he admitted, almost relieved Domenico knew at least that much.

"Still away then?" Domenico added letting Lucreto know he was well aware of the situation.

"Yes," Lucreto whispered. "Away and being treated. She just...."

His throat became clogged, and his eyes strained. He bowed his head and stared at the floor. He had come to this meeting determined not to succumb to whatever Domenico had in mind. But now it seemed like this might be an opportunity to get out from under the incredible dent his sister's illness had put in his finances. He had been wondering how he could continue to live the life-style he had become accustomed to and keep his sister safely away from the city and the prying eyes of his associates and influential neighbors.

Though he had known all along, Domenico nodded his head as if it had suddenly dawned on him what Lucreto wanted in return for agreeing to his request, "It is a matter of money, isn't it? Money for treatment, money for... discretion?"

"You would not expose my poor sister's unfortunate situation?" Lucreto said, pain and fear in his voice.

"I would, but there is really no need. As a matter of fact, I and my associates certainly *would* advance you enough for your needs, under the appropriate conditions," Domenico said knowing he had Lucreto right where he wanted him.

The two men sat in silence for a few moments as Domenico gave the doctor time to consider his options, though there really were not any viable ones open to him. Domenico knew how much Lucreto enjoyed his upper class prestige and lifestyle. He had discreetly looked into the doctor's life for a weakness he could use for bargaining power long before he invited the man to his office. In his position as Secretary of State, he had also used his authority to demand a report on the pontiff's health from the Vatican doctor.

He was not at all concerned about what appeared to be the doctor's reluctance to comply with his request. In fact he had expected it knowing it would come down to financial incentive. The added advantage of knowing something the good doctor wanted kept a secret just added to the assurance the doctor would not only comply, but do so in a discreet and convincing way.

Lucreto sat with his head still cast down, eyes fixed on the soft, quietly geometrically patterned carpet. When he finally spoke, it was very slowly, as though in a trance.

"The Holy Father needs a vacation," he said, giving the Secretary of State his medical report.

Domenico leaned back and smiled.

"Do have a cognac before you leave, Doctore," he said as a way of calming the now totally submissive Lucreto.

After Dr. Lucreto left, Domenico started working at his desk, but it was not long before he heard the familiar syncopated pattern of four knocks on his door. He laughed to himself as he got up to admit Alfredo Gianfredo, the papal valet. He had known Alfredo since they were children in Naples. In fact, Domenico had gotten Alfredo his job here in the Vatican.

"Ah, Alfredo. Welcome," he said.

"Ah...eh...Your Grace—ah—Your *Eminence*, you are so fortunate to have my company," laughed the almost arrogant valet.

"Yes, yes, Alfredo. The joke is getting old my friend," Domenico said as he restrained his annoyance at the man's obvious lack of creativity. "A glass of wine?"

"What a question!" Alfredo responded.

Domenico went to a small cabinet near the window, bent down, and took out two wine glasses and a bottle of red Capri.

"Sit down and rest that boney body of yours," Domenico said. "Let's see if we can raise some flesh on it."

"Mille grazie," said Gianfredo, taking the glass and holding it up to the window, letting the afternoon sunlight shine through it.

"Mmm, superb color," he said knowing Domenico always had the best. "A toast, Domenico. To the days of our foolish youth, the days in the canteen. Do you remember those days, Domenico? The back streets of Naples?"

"You will never change, will you? No matter what," Domenico laughed in spite of himself.

Alfredo Gianfredo was one of the few people who knew all about Domenico's past. He was also one of the few people he could be relaxed with. Though this man knew a lot about him, Domenico was confident his friend would not betray him. He had made sure Alfredo was well taken care of and comfortable though at times he was arrogant above his position as papal valet.

"I say, a toast to our...enterprise," Domenico said as he raised his glass.

"Our enterprise," laughed Alfredo and raised his glass high above his head. "Ah yes! The enterprise which will reform the world. The enterprise which shall be the salvation of the future. The enterprise which...."

"My God, you sound like a common play actor," Domenico interrupted his friend laughing at his dramatic antics.

"Well, why not? I am going to be playacting all the time in a few days, eh?" Alfredo said as he downed some of his wine.

"Incorrigible fool is what you are!" laughed Domenico trying hard to act disgusted by his friend's antics.

"I will be good at it, too," Alfredo added. "Believe me."

"You had better be, my friend. A lot rides on your performance," Domenico said more seriously. "Now, what about Sister Simione?"

"Ah, yes! Our illustrious papal cook," Alfredo said with a wink of his eye. "I do not think she will be a problem. She wants nothing more than to please the Holy Father. I will keep her out of touch with Luciano—oh—pardon me, 'His Holiness,' as much as possible."

"Alfredo, one of these days...."

Alfredo laughed broadly, "Poor Domenico, you worry too much! Believe me, things are pretty well under control."

"Pretty well? Pretty well?" Domenico roared, all of his pent up emotions letting loose in front of his friend, "Pretty well is not good enough!"

"Dio! There you go again," Alfredo stopped laughing realizing he had pushed his friend too far.

"Quiet, you idiot!" Domenico spouted still out of control, "Everything has to be perfect—it has got to be perfect!"

Alfredo, took another sip of his wine giving Domenico time to calm down. He had seen this type of sudden explosion before. He knew the stress the last several months had been on Domenico. He also knew the man was meticulously careful and had every piece of the puzzle firmly in place.

"Nothing is perfect, Domenico," he said quietly as he continued to sip his wine.

"God is perfect," said Domenico as he slowly regained his composure.

All that he had put in place was for the good of the church. He truly felt he was doing it all for the church.

"Yes," Alfredo whispered almost under his breath. "*Only* God!"

By the time Gianfredo left, it was already getting dark. Domenico went to have a light meal and quickly returned to his chambers. He poured himself an Ausbach Uralt and settled comfortably in his preferred arm chair. He let his muscles relax and his mind clear. He could easily have dozed off were it not for the fact that he expected still another visitor, a very special visitor before he could call it a day. It had been a busy day full of meetings. It was a day when he finally saw all that he had planned come together. The puzzle was nearly completed.

His special visitor was coming not only for intimate personal reasons, but also, now, for political ones. He heard Luciano Steidler's soft knock and got up quickly to let him in.

"Buona sera, Luciano," he said, holding a hand on each of the young man's smooth biceps. "You are looking well."

"A bit tired, perhaps," Luciano said removing the cape that was part of his military uniform. "I just came off duty."

"Yes, yes, of course. I know," Domenico said sympathetically. "Come, have an Ausbach with me. You will feel better."

Domenico handed him a glass of brandy, and they sat down opposite one another.

"So, tell me, then," said Domenico, "what is happening among the guards these days?"

"Nothing special," Luciano said quietly. "Things are pretty quiet. That can sometimes be more tiring than dealing with a band of terrorists trying to break in."

Luciano shook his head as if to dust off the dull strain of the day. His straight, long blond hair whisked about his young face. The first things one noticed about Luciano were his hair and eyes, especially his eyes. They were as large and round as those of a two year old and sparkled with a hint of light blue. He had a clean look about him, fresh, like the icy air of the Austrian altitudes in which he was raised. When draped in Michelangelo's famous multi-colored striped uniform, Luciano was a magnet for feminine attention.

"And how are you?" Luciano asked Domenico knowing he had planned many meetings today.

"Tired also, my friend," Domenico admitted. "It has been a long, but profitable day."

He leaned forward, toward Luciano, and said confidentially, "Things will soon be ready for you. His Holiness will be taking a short vacation in Ortesei, if things go according to plan."

"The meetings went well today then?" Luciano asked. "It is while His Holiness in on vacation that it will happen?"

"Yes," Domenico answered shaking his head. "Are you afraid?"

"No. I believe in what we are doing," Luciano assured him, "I know you will guide me throughout the whole process."

"You can be sure about that," Domenico added reassuringly. "Still, I detect a certain uncertainty in you. What is it, eh?"

Luciano hesitated, "Well, I am perhaps concerned about carrying out the deception effectively. I do not want to disappoint you or jeopardize the mission."

"You need not be concerned, dear Luciano. The resemblance between you and the pontiff is very strong. We just need a little theatrical expertise to make you a bit older," Domenico said as he turned the young man's face side to side as if confirming the striking resemblance between Luciano and the pontiff. "Also, we intend to keep Monsignor Maestoso and Sister Simione as far from you as possible. They would be the only ones who might detect a difference."

Domenico finished his brandy, and put the glass down slowly on a delicate table next to his chair.

"Now," he said, "are you concerns dealt with? Will you stay here tonight?"

Luciano's face muscles tightened as if he was straining to control some deeply hidden secret or emotion, "I don't know…"

"Oh?" Domenico said softly, correctly interpreting the young man's physical movements. "Something is still wrong?"

"There is something else, something I have been wanting to tell you for a long time," Luciano confessed quietly.

Domenico leaned back. He had actually been expecting the young man's confession for some time now. It was good that it was going to come out into the open before the deception began.

"Well, then," Domenico suggested, "Isn't it best that you tell me now so you are not distracted in your upcoming role in our plan?"

Luciano looked up at Domenico, studying his face, wondering if he already knew. Domenico's reputation for reading people's thoughts was well known among his staff. They all had found out, some the hard way, it was never good to try and lie or keep something from this powerful man.

"I ...I..." Luciano stuttered still trying to find the right way to begin this awkward though necessary confession.

"Come now, Luciano," Domenico encouraged him. "After everything we have been to each other, I do not have to play the solicitous confessor with you, do I?"

Not getting the response he was looking for, Domenico stepped into his previous role of a priest receiving the confession of a wayward saint.

In a deep, mocking voice he asked, "What was it my son? A sin of impurity?"

Luciano feigned a smile, fully aware of the irony of what Domenico had just said.

"Yes," he said, "you might regard it as such. The fact is, for some months now I have been with a woman."

"Good!" Domenico said with resounding conviction. "I wanted you to have that experience."

"You, what?" Luciano responded in wonderment and surprise.

"Well, what did you expect from me?" Domenico asked. "Jealousy? Shock? Bah! You should know me better than that. Actually, I have expected this for some time. It is perfectly natural, isn't it, for a handsome young man like yourself to draw the attentions of a woman?"

"Natural? For me?" Luciano asked in shock and confusion, "For men like us?"

"Of course! Just what do you think *my* days of youth were like?" Domenico countered revealing a little of his past Luciano had not heard before. "Believe me, I am happy this has happened for you."

Luciano looked at him with wonder and affection. This man had never ceased to amaze him. The more he got to know him the more he admired him.

"Now tell me about her," Domenico said, surprising the young man even more. "Is she Italian?"

"No, a foreigner. She is from Bulgaria," Luciano explained almost excitedly. "And she writes verses! She is very young, about twenty-two, I think. Her name is Ma...."

"A Bulgarian poetess," Domenico interrupted. "Good Lord! What did you say her name was?"

"Maria, Maria Penkova," Luciano smiled. "She is very sensitive and very loving."

"Sounds interesting," Domenico commented, writing down the woman's name even as he went on to say, "Of course, once you have assumed your role, this affair will have to be carefully controlled."

"I am not sure I know how to do that," Luciano said reflectively.

"You can leave that to me, Luciano," Domenico quietly assured him. "I will take care of it, I promise you."

"Thank you," Luciano answered quietly. "I should have known you would understand and be able to take care of everything. I am sorry I did not tell you this sooner."

Domenico remained silent for a moment.

"No apology necessary," he said, then added, "You are staying tonight, then?"

Luciano was silent for a moment or two, and then he looked directly at Domenico and said softly, "Yes, of course I will stay."

Chapter 3

Execution of the Plan

bout one week later, just as Domenico had calculated, Pope Pius XIII was leaning well back in a soft seat on his private jet headed for Milan. His confessor and friend of many years, Father Vitttorio Santo, S. J., was seated next to him by the window. The pontiff disliked window seats although he enjoyed flying. At first he thought he would never get accustomed to it. He was not one to experiment much with new things or ideas, something many of his staff were well aware of, often to their dismay and frustration. When he assumed the papacy, he had pledged himself to the upholding of traditional values. Domenico degli Alfieri, a frustrating man whom Pius thought very highly of despite their ideological differences, had tried to persuade him to be more flexible in his views. As he leaned back in his seat, he reflected on the conversations he had recently had with his highly qualified Secretary of State.

"The world has changed a great deal, Your Holiness, and will change even more," degli Alfieri had said. "The church must change with it if it is to survive."

"Survival is under the care of the Lord," Pius replied. "No matter what we do, the church remains. History has taught us that time and time again."

"Yes, but just think of the speed with which things are happening today. It has no historical precedent. The computer revolution has even changed the way people think. Psychology has become a new science...."

"Was it ever a science at all?" laughed Pius.

His attempt at levity totally wasted on his ever serious advisor, Domenico continued with his attempt to convince Pius of his need for change, "With all due respect, Holiness, intellectual life is different today. People behave

23

differently as a result. This new sexual upheaval, for example, the prominence of varied sexual preferences...."

"Please! I will have no more talk of this," Pius remembered saying more passionately than he had intended.

He immediately felt bad about the outburst and consciously calmed his mind, "I will tell you what is happening, Domenico. It is unquestionably true that there are more sick people in the world today than ever before in the history of mankind. However, I believe the reason is a loss of faith in traditional values. Changing tradition to try and keep up with modern mindsets is not the way to bring more people into the church family. But what I do see is that in this computer age, as you call it, the media over-communicates and gives us such on the spot reports that we hear and see more about such happenings. Thus we are getting the impression that the world is much worse off than it really is."

"And what about the political situation?" Domenico added, trying once again to show Pius what he considered to be the true nature of the world outside the Vatican walls.

Pius always enjoyed these interchanges with Domenico knowing it would stimulate a healthy interchange between them, "What about it? We must continue to fight for the religious freedom of our oppressed brethren and pray for the conversion of their diabolical governments. If only there were more prayer—more prayer and more sacrifice."

"Why talk of fighting?" Domenico had asked. "Isn't there such a thing as negotiation anymore? Is it necessary to always remain so rigid in our stance? Is not cooperation possible in this ever changing world we live in?"

"Cooperation or compromise?" Pius countered realizing he needed to bring this interchange to an end before either of them got really angry. "Can one 'cooperate' with Satan?"

The pope shook his head as he recalled how angrily Domenico had marched out of his office. Staring passed Vittorio into the clouds rushing by outside, he realized degli Alfieri's ideas were definitely not to his liking. One thing he was confident of though was that his Secretary of State's primary concern was for the betterment of the holy church. He was a very efficient and intelligent, and in his heart he was devoted to Christ's work.

Suddenly realizing how even thinking of that conversation with Domenico had agitated him, he thought perhaps Dr. Lucreto had been right after all. Pius had argued with him at the suggestion of a short break to get away to the mountains, but now that he was on his way a glow of carefree relaxation had begun to take hold.

His Holiness smiled. It would be good to once again be immersed in the spectacular silence of the Dolomite Mountains. Even now he remembered how those massive limestone peaks sheer facades glowed multicolored in the sunset. He would get in some skiing, too, he thought happily. Of course, he would thoroughly enjoy the change in food and wine which leaned distinctly toward the German there, especially at Martha's.

"You know, Vittorio," Pius said to his trusted friend, "I am actually pleased to be getting away and looking forward to resting at your sister's place again."

"And perhaps, Holiness, also to the best speck to be found in all the Trentino?" Father Santo smiled gently.

The pope could not resist smiling in return, as he admitted, "The speck had occurred to me, I must confess."

What a magnificent human being this Father Santo is, thought Pius. *He is the soul embodiment of amiability*. Physically, the good Father reminded Pius of degli Alfieri—tall and sinewy, but his disposition was entirely different. One could feel the holiness project, as it were, from Father Santo. He was a priest functioning in the world, yet living as though he were behind the walls of a monastery. He had many published writings to his credit, not the least important of which was his latest paper, "Asceticism in the Modern World: A Viable Alternative?"

Father Santo smiled as he realized Pius was indeed beginning to relax. His sister Martha and her husband, Wilhem Franken, had bought a small lodge in Ortisei some years ago. It was called "Martha's." Vittorio knew without a doubt Pius could be at ease there while maintaining considerable privacy.

"The only thing that concerns me a bit," said Father Santo, "is the current increase in terrorist activities."

"Ah, yes. I do not suppose the issue of sovereignty for that area will ever be settled. But look, we have nothing to worry about. I have five of my best guards with me," Pius pointed out. "They will be on the lookout for disturbances whether we are on the sloops or in the dining room."

"You are satisfied that things can be left in degli Alfieri's hands for a while?" Father Santo asked hoping his friend could truly relax while he was here in the mountains.

"Yes, dear Vittorio," Pius smiled, "Though degli Alfieri represents a most important component in my staff—the loyal opposition, I have every confidence in him."

"Then we shall say no more about it," smiled Vittorio. "In fact, the Vatican is something we will not mention again—for a while anyhow."

"I like that idea, my friend," Pius agreed. "But my mind will not let me forget everything. I am thinking of using some of the time to outline a new encyclical. In fact it will be based on your last paper, 'Asceticism in the Modern World: A Viable Alternative?'"

"You are joking," Vittorio exclaimed, pleasantly surprised by the pontiff's statement.

"Not at all," laughed Pius enjoying the fact that he had surprised and pleased his longtime friend. "You have something important to say in your work, and I would like to bring it to a wider audience if you have no objections."

Father Santo curled his lips in a smile in his own especially pleasant way, "I am very flattered."

Vittorio was fifteen years older than Pius, and some facial grooves were beginning to appear. *Somehow*, Pius thought, *they just made his face more pleasant looking—kinder. The wrinkles around his mouth seemed to smile when he smiled. I pray I age as gracefully!*

In a few minutes, Pius felt his ears clog and he knew they had begun their descent for Milan. He looked out the window as the plane banked and made a descending turn toward the airport. He felt the engines as they were slowed, he could see the flaps on the wings lowered, and soon the white strip was speeding beneath them. Pius realized he had been holding his breath as they touched down a bit roughly, but came to a smooth stop.

Private limousines were waiting for them at the terminal to take Pius and his party to Ortisei. His leaving the Vatican had not been publicized, so there were not any crowds for which Pius was very grateful. He enjoyed his public role, but all too often his private times of rest and relaxation were invaded by unwanted reporters or the notorious and often annoying paparazzi.

Despite the rather lengthy drive, Pius began to feel even more relaxed. The limousine was very comfortable, and when they got to Balzano and picked up the Great Dolomite Road, he realized he had forgotten how startling beautiful the scenery could be. The highway, a marvel of modern engineering, hair-pinned its way through spectacular mountain passes providing views of the Marmolada and other massifs which were unique to this area. Pius thoroughly enjoyed the view though the driver, appearing as though he hardly noticed the show, kept a steady speed on all but the sharpest curves.

Arriving at the famous mountaineering town of Canazei and the Prodoi Pass, they turned north for Ortisei. They passed through town on the way to Martha's, cheerfully viewing the quaint woodworkers' shops for which the place is famous. It was a sunny, crisp day, and perhaps for the first time, Pius noticed the air. The car window was opened a bit, and he inhaled slowly and deeply. It was pure and fresh, and made him realize how polluted Rome had become. Once again he silently thanked Dr. Lucreto for suggesting he come for this time of refreshing. He must remember to express his gratitude to the good doctor when they return.

The car turned left and began the ascent up a short, steep hill to the small chalet that was their final destination. Martha came hurrying out of the door and lovingly embraced her brother. Then she turned respectfully to Pius.

"Welcome, Your Holiness. We are honored once again to have you join us," she said sincerely.

"Shh," said Pius putting two fingers to his lips and looking around as if the paparazzi were hiding behind every snow bank.

Martha smiled pleasantly, "Ah! Who is there to hear us way out here, Your Holiness, the snow banks?"

Martha's husband, Franken, a big man in stature but quiet in nature, came out to join them. With a courteous nod toward his guests, he helped with the luggage, handling the heavy bags as though they were toys. Pius was truly thankful for these two wonderful servants of the Lord.

Pius and his group spent the afternoon settling in and getting some rest before dinner. Martha had prepared a wonderful hearty meal of speck dumplings, sausages, and eggplant, accompanied by several liters of Santa Magdalena. Pius was indeed very glad he had taken his doctor's advice and agreed to this short reprieve before the upcoming audience. Perhaps he would introduce some of Vittorio's ideas at the audience.

Franken, knowing Pius' love for skiing, interrupted the pontiff's thoughts and said, "Skiing should be very good tomorrow. It is dry and just perfect for some great downhill maneuvers."

"What do you say, Vittorio," Pius asked his friend, "shall we try it?"

"Yes, I think so," smiled Vittorio, knowing full well Pius could out maneuver him on the slopes though it was a joy to watch the pontiff relax and enjoy himself at something he so obviously loved doing.

"Good!" said Pius, glad his friend would join him on the slopes.

They all slept well and started out early the next morning. Franken had gone ahead with their skis, and the group of guards followed closely behind them, ever alert for a potential threat or an unwanted interruption. They all rode a cable car to the summit of one of the expert slopes where Franken was waiting for them.

"All ready for you, Signori, Mein Herren," Franken said respectfully, standing with the skis upright, heels set in the snow.

Franken helped each of his guests into their skis as they prepared for an invigorating run down the expert slope before them. Pius waited as Franken assisted Vittorio, thoroughly enjoying the wonder around him. What a spectacle the Lord had put together for them this beautiful day! Besides its visual delights, the mountain had a sound of its own, and a smell of freshness unsurpassed anywhere else in the world. As he readied his skis, Pius relished the cushioned softness under foot. Franken had been right. The snow conditions were perfect! It was going to be an exceptional day!

Here at the top of this beautiful mountain, there was no Vatican, no cardinals, and no politics to interfere with his day. There was only the simplest of spiritual communions and it was his; all under his control. His Venetian parents had seen to it that he started skiing as a child, and that had strongly contributed to the expertise and confidence he had today.

He was more than ready. He looked straight ahead, assumed a balanced position, and let go with his poles. A few moments later, Father Santo started down behind him. The guards took a faster traverse closer to the fall line to keep their important responsibilities in close range and view. They knew, of course, of the pontiff's skill on the ski slope. They were more concerned with unwanted and unwelcomed intruders as they were out in the open and exposed here on the side of the great mountain.

Pius was oblivious to his guards concern as he maneuvered a ski inward a fraction, shifted weight, and started his turns: rotation, lift, swing, and a flowing arc formed in the snow as he changed direction. Skis parallel once more, he streaked across the fall line and started a turn in the opposite direction, connecting his trail to another smooth arc as he leaned slightly into the turn. Across again, turn again, and down, always down. Whole body working, rhythmically coordinated, alert but intense, poles swept back, skis hissing, and wind, everywhere wind, his face pushing through a funnel of air.

As he neared the bottom, he noticed a long, level run at the end of the slope. His heart-beat quickened as he swung into the fall line and flexed his knees in a schuss position. The wind rammed his face, whirring in his ears as he accelerated. Faster, skis roaring over snow, trees flashing in the corner of an eye, slope speeding under him. A numbness took over his spirit. He was flying in a void.

When he swished onto the level run, he returned to earth. Pointing skis inward and pressing the edges down a bit, he slowed his approach. Then, with a forceful but flowing lift and twist, he turned completely around to the right. Skis across his path of motion now, he edged them well into the snow, spewing up a plume of white granules as he slid to a controlled stop.

Father Santo soon approached, more slowly, of course, and came to a halt at his side. They looked at each other and smiled. Both knew this was great for the mind, body, and spirit!

That was exhilarating, Pius thought, but it was on his next run that Pius really warmed up and felt that special euphoria unique to skiing. He took a

faster traverse and descended swiftly, tracing out an impressive series of parallel turns and carrying a gushing fountain of froth. First to the right, then to
the left, then right again. He leaned effortlessly into each turn, living turns that
had a tempo of their own. He needed no thought, no calculation. He was the
skis, the slope, the wind, the sun…the universe.

His exhilaration, however, was to last only a few moments longer. As soon
as Santo drew up next to him, one of the guards sped toward them.

"I am Luciano Steidler, Your Holiness," he said. "There appears to be a
band of men approaching on the right. It does not look good. Allow me to
escort you in the opposite direction while the others divert them."

Pius looked around in the distance and confirmed Luciano's information.
He agreed to go with him, and the three started to move rapidly away.

"There is a steilhang just ahead," Luciano shouted. "We can schuss down
and be clear of this area."

Pius looked ahead and saw what looked more like the edge of a cliff rather
than the top of a steep racing trail. Concerned but trusting in the guard beside
him, they all pushed on faster towards this point. Suddenly, they found themselves surrounded by a dozen giants. It was an ambush!

These men were all dressed exactly the same and wore brown face masks.
They had come upon them swiftly from all directions and were drawing their
circle closer to completely surround them. One of the big men went boldly up
to Pius.

"You will come with us," he said with authority, his voice deep, gruff, and
Slavic.

Father Santo's temples were pulsating, his body one electrified nerve. How
did this happen? When had they become so vulnerable? Where were the rest
of the guards?

Pius looked directly at the man in front of him and said, "Suppose I refuse?"

The man gestured to two of the others who grasped the pontiff's arms.
Then the first man tore the pole straps from Pius wrists, making him totally at
the mercy of his captors.

Santo, his blood surging in the furnace of his veins, crazed by the blas-
phemy he had just witnessed against the pope, made a furious jump toward the
men. The end of a pole swung sharply into his chest almost as it had appeared
out of nowhere. Surprised and gasping for breath, Vittorio started sliding back-
wards toward the steilhang. His mind, jumping into survival mode, told him he
could regain control. He would turn around, he thought, race down the slope,
and get help for Pius. He was feeling the bite of a wild beast on his breast as
the pole continued to do damage to his inner organs, but he managed to bring
himself into a ready position as he went over the edge.

But there was no trail. There was nothing to receive his ready skis. As he looked below him there was nothing but the bottom of a ravine far below him.

"God forgive me," he called out as he sank into the crevice.

Suddenly, he was not falling anymore. He was floating. He was floating on his back in the warm waters of the Mediterranean; floating with Anna at his side. Anna whom he had betrayed.

"God forgive me," he prayed as he thought of dear Anna.

Then he was in one of his classes in the seminary, the one given by a professor he had come to hate.

"God forgive me," he whispered as he repented of his dislike for one God had placed in authority over him.

"God...God help me!" he prayed as he continued his seemingly endless descent into the deadly ravine below.

Just before he reached the bottom, he saw his writings, scholars reading them, using them. He was thankful his work would go on to the next generations. He felt a bishop's hands on his head, remembered how he had lived through his first mass though he had been incredibly nervous. He thought about all of the confessions he had heard over the years, many confessions, and finally raised his right hand in absolution of Pius XIII.

Sleep.
Down and sleep.
Rest.
Down to rest.
Peace.
Down in peace.
Down, sleep, rest, peace.
Amen.

It must have been many hours later when Pius finally awoke from a drug induced sleep. He felt the warmth of sunshine on the bed as he slowly, almost painfully opened his eyes. The first thing he noticed once his eyes could focus was that one window of the small room was shut and barred, but he could still look out onto a village street. He knew for sure he was no longer in Italy. All the clues he could see from his window said he was in France. In fact, muffled as they were, the voices he managed to hear were distinctively of southern France.

Pius tried to clear his mind, still foggy from the drugs they must have given him to keep him asleep and hidden as they transported him here. He began to remember. Vittorio, oh my God, Vittorio! Tears flowed from his tired eyes as he recalled the old priest's scream as he went over the cliff. Why? What was happening? Who were his imprisoners?

He felt too dazed to remain standing. He sat down hard realizing his head was spinning. The drugs were still making him groggy. He stretched out on his back on the bed, and stared at a blank white ceiling as he tried to make some sense of what was happening.

Lord, what is your plan in all this? Show me the way. There must be a purpose behind this disaster, for you always have a purpose. This is the center of my faith and I will trust in you.

Then, in his stupor of sadness, he recited the third psalm, and slept once more.

During the days of captivity to come, he was to watch and listen very carefully, but to no avail. No one, neither the guard at the door nor the peasant woman who brought his food, would say a word to him. Obviously they had been instructed to keep him safe but away from anyone who might recognize and report his whereabouts. Was anyone looking for him? Did anyone even know he had been abducted? Surely his guards had reported what had happened! And what of Vittorio's body? Martha, oh, poor dear Martha! She must be grieving terribly! She and Vittorio had been so close! Did she even know?

In the meantime, Domenico degli Alfieri continued to implement ever part of his meticulous plan. He finally had reached Martha on the telephone once he knew she had been made aware of Vittorio's untimely death.

"We thought it best," Domenico said to Martha, "to bring His Holiness back immediately after what happened. He is out of his mind with grief over the untimely death of your dear brother. I want you to know that I, too, am very saddened by the awful accident. Your brother was one of God's greatest. I assure you that a representative will be sent to the memorial services. Please make sure you let us know when they will be held."

Martha whimpered, unable to respond to the Secretary of State.

"Be of good faith, Martha," Domenico comforted her. "What more can I say to you? The Lord has his own reasons. Just know we all respected and loved your brother. He will be missed here at the Vatican where he dedicated so much of his time."

"Thank....thank you," Martha tried to respond. "He was such a good...."

She cried loudly, gasping for breath. Alfieri promised to pray for him and her, and hung up. Actually the receiver slipped out of his moist hand. He felt so empty. When he thought of Luciano's description of the way it happened, he could plunge a knife into that stupid brute who caused it. Soviet bastards! How could this have happened? He told them no one was to be injured! He told them it was imperative they stick to the plan! Maybe this meant they were to abort the whole thing. Was this God's way of telling them the plan was faulty? Maybe he need to reevaluate.

But no, it was too late to pull out. Everything else had gone well. In just a few days, Pius XIII will be having an audience, and the Church will begin to move in its new direction. Vittorio Santo's death was part of the price to be paid. My God—what a price it was, but Vittorio's death would not be in vain! His death would mark the new era of church discipline!

Chapter 4

Carlo Maestoso

After persuading, as only he could persuade, degli Alfieri's secretary to slip his note under the door, Carlo Maestoso wondered if his impetuosity had caused him to do something stupid. Wouldn't it have been better to take degli Alfieri and his group completely by surprise? Of course it would have, and yet…it was and always had been this way with him.

As he looked back on it now, the action he had taken many years ago when he first struck out on his own was an impetuous one. It had led him to many valuable experiences that eventually led him to where he was today. So, yes, it was the right thing to do back then and it was also the right thing to do now. Though it might put degli Alfieri on alert, showing an opponent that you have information that could thwart their plan without telling them what it was often led them to reveal parts that were yet unknown, though perhaps necessary for the counter plan now in play.

Yes, they would prevail. Carlo was sure of it. He and his loyal friends would confront degli Alfieri and his bogus pope on their way to the audience. They would not allow the masquerade to move farther than the courtyard. They must not be allowed to move into the Piazza S. Pietro. The real Pius XIII was now in hiding in Castel S. Angelo. The plan was to bring him in at the exact moment through the narrow "passetto" between the castle and the Vatican, oust the imposter, and return Pius to his divinely ordained place prior to entering the audience chamber. Though a conflict could be expected as the two factions met, the element of surprise should prevent anyone being seriously injured. That was the hope and prayer of them all.

It was little more than a week ago when Carlo had first become suspicious. He and Pius had been personal friends for a long time so they knew each other very well. Carlo, who was some thirty years older, had been one of Pius' teachers in the seminary. A very close friendship developed to the point that now they thought of themselves as related, perhaps uncle and nephew. Now it seemed like he was being obstructed from seeing his former pupil in private. He knew his friend was upset by the untimely death of his friend, Father Santo, but his time of mourning would not exclude another close friend. No, instead Pius would have most definitely sent for him long before this.

But it was because of the discriminating taste buds of his friend that really clinched it for Carlo. Carlo's palate had begun its training at an early age to the point he could no longer be deceived by chefs who thought they could substitute false seasonings into an already perfected recipe. His training started when he was working in his father's restaurant in Trastevere when he was thirteen. The senior Carlo put him through the many phases of the business: dishwasher, clean-up man, busboy, waiter, and finally assistant chef. It was in this last position that Carlo began to find the direction he wanted for his life.

Antonio, the chef under whom Carlo had to work, was known to be a difficult man with the temperament of a major artist. Despite his gruffness, however, Carlo thrived as his assistant. He learned remarkably fast for one so young, and he learned well, even though Antonio would never display the slightest hint of praise of approval. In fact the aging chef began to think of Carlo as his protégé.

However, the day of Antonio's sister's funeral revealed the arrogant chef's true nature and proved to be a turning point for Carlo. Though it was really not unexpected, the news came that the master chef was not up to coming to work. Some said he had been drinking a lot. In any case, he eventually did show up, but was not up to fixing some of his signature dishes such as the Fettuccine Bolognese. He had asked Carlo to prepare the meal for him and went to rest in one of the small offices off the kitchen area. The truth was, the man was difficult enough when he was sober. Today, in his drunken condition, he was intolerable. They were all relieved when the man decided to find a place to sleep in off for a while.

Later, Pietro Campanello, one of the restaurant's steady customers, called the senior Carlo to his table after finishing his meal. Always the gracious host, the senior Carlo quickly answered his favored guest's request.

"Senor Maestoso," Pietro said. "You know that I have been eating here for years."

Carlo senior bowed his head in acknowledgment of his appreciation for such loyalty.

"Let me tell you," Pietro continued, "I have never tasted the fettuccine the way it was prepared today. Never! It was magnificent!"

"It is true," several other customers near Pietro's table chimed in.

"Viva il Chef!" many also added in their praise for the seemingly new level of expertise Carlo senior's kitchen chef had reached this day.

"Come," Pietro said waving his arms to include all of those agreeing with his evaluation of the meal, "Bring your chef out for a bow. This meal is beyond extraordinary today!"

Everyone working in the kitchen knew the truth, but unfortunately the senior Carlo did not. So it was Antonio who walked out of the kitchen — or did he stagger out? It all depended on who you talked to that was there that day. Antonio gladly received the acclamation, possibly even thinking he deserved it since he had trained the young Carlo so well!

Although the young Carlo was quite unwilling to make a scene and enlighten the clientele, his innards were rebelling against the deception perpetrated at his expense. There was a sound within him, a voice that would not allow him to be comfortable with this situation, the masquerade, the injustice made him unable to rest. That very night, he gathered together the little money he had managed to save, held his father in a farewell embrace, and was on his way to other pastures.

He went north, of course. Everyone knew it was in the north that opportunities walked up to you on the street and shook your hands. He wanted to be cooking again, and perhaps after saving enough he would open his own place. But, as with so many young dreamers, that was not the way it was going to be. After reaching Milano and being shunted from one kitchen to another, gaining more experience, more expertise, and more weight with each job, he found himself unemployed one morning and in the office of the Compagnie Internationale des Wagons Lits, the owner/operators of the Orient Express.

He was not sure what he was doing there. True, they had advertised for chefs, but he could not imagine any kind of sophisticated cuisine could be served or even desired on board a rickety, rocking, smelly, noisy train! Perhaps the romance of travel had appealed to his youthful spirit of twenty-five years or maybe it was the idea of always being on the go, seeing different places, some rather exotic, meeting strange people. Whatever it was something had caused him to make his way here to this place.

The attractive receptionist smiled at him curtly and said, "Signore Carozza will see you now."

Interesting how women seemed different here, not at all like the Romans, he thought. The Eternal City was also a modern, busy metropolis, but here the "strictly business" attitude, the comportment, a certain...coolness. Was it a façade? Carlo was already getting very good at recognizing falseness. It was an ability that would grow steadily as he experienced more of life; an ability which was to serve him later in a matter of the greatest importance.

"Grazie," he said as she led him through the office door.

Signore Carozza was obviously a pipe-smoker, if not a pipe-nut! On his desk, where one might expect to find piles of papers, he had clusters of pipes of all varieties. On the wall behind his desk chair was a painting, more likely a print, in color, of a huge calabash. There were pipes strategically placed at various points around the office: two on an end table next to a black leather couch; two small black ones and a brown thrown together on a cocktail table in front of the couch. Others sat on the window sill where there also were five or six apothecary jars filled with different blends of tobacco.

He was puffing away as Carlo walked in, drawing deeply on a long, curved-stem model, perhaps of Bulgarian origin. The flame on the end of a long match dipped at regular intervals into the bowl, keeping rhythm with his breathing. His face seemed to be continually obscured by a meandering curtain of smoke.

He put the match down and extended his right hand to Carlo, "Buon girono, Signor' Maestoso."

"Buon girono."

"Please, have a seat," Carozza said, indicating the couch.

He took a chair facing the couch, while Carlo sat on the couch behind the cocktail table.

"I will not take any more of your time than necessary," Carozza said. "But first tell me, how much do you know about the Orient Express?"

"Nothing at all, really," admitted Carlo.

"Good," Carozza puffed energetically. "Then I do not have to be concerned if my brief introduction is not completely accurate."

He leaned back, drew deeply on his pipe, and continued, "For the past ten years or so, we have been running a sophisticated service from Paris to Istanbul, and there are expansion plans being considered all the time. Ignoring the other routes, for the moment, our principal run east starts at the Gare de Lyon in Paris. From there we move on to Dijon, Lausanne, in Switzerland, through the Simplon tunnel to Milano, and on to Verona, Venezia, Trieste, Ljubjana, Zagreb, Belgrad, Sofia, and Istanbul."

As Carozza spoke he waved his arms around as if indicating the stops the train made on an imaginary map between the two of them.

"We have felt the need for some time now for a better dining atmosphere on this train," Carozza explained. "We need more innovative menus, more tastily prepared food, etc. We have already hired Signor' Farid el Khwarizmi, a pastry chef from Damascus, who is also very capable in Turkish cuisine."

His mention of Farid came as if he thought Carlo would immediately recognize the name of the famous pastry chef. Carlo nodded as if to agree with this assumption though in truth he had never heard of the pastry chef.

"Now, Signore, let me not mince words. You come very highly recommended, and I know you have very diversified experience. The job of Principal Chef on this train is yours if you want it."

Carlo jumped up as if Carozza had unexpectedly hit him in the back of the head. Had they confused him with someone else? It was possible, he supposed, but the diversified part was definitely true. He was intrigued enough to give it a try.

"Very well then," Carlo answered. "I shan't mince words either. I will take it providing the salary is appropriate."

He added the last phrase almost as an afterthought, surprising himself at having uttered it. Carozza seemed genuinely relieved. They came to quick agreement regarding remuneration and Carlo began his career on the Orient Express. For about the next nine years, up to the first rumblings of a second great war, Carlo Maestoso worked as a chef on the Orient Express. He became a master during this time, learning from Farid as well as developing from his own experiences. He tasted things all the time. Most often, his meals consisted of all the tasting he did. He seldom needed a full meal. This worked wonders for his palate, but not for his figure.

However, it was not only a taste for food that developed further during this time. The train had a life of its own. It breathed through the dining car and evacuated at the caboose. Its heartbeat was the unrelenting pulse of the engine. Its corridors formed its bloodstream, veins filled with all kinds of corpuscles: the tightly compressed ones at the beginning of the run through France; the neat units from Switzerland; the gay, disorderly ones through Italy and Yugoslavia; the stiff, militant corpuscles in Bulgari; and the loud, bundle-lugging passengers at the Turkish end.

Then there were three plump corpuscles that Carlo began to notice more and more. The "madonnas of the sleeping cars," they came to be called.

"Carmelina, I love you," could be heard in all the accents of Europe. She was one of the three young women who regularly made the run and was always happy with a ready response. She and her companions were rarely seen outside of a sleeping car during the trip from Paris to Venice. Carlo was convinced they even *ate* in bed. When Carmelina did walk the corridors, people always wondered who this gypsy was. She dressed and flirted like a gypsy.

However, Farid would say, "She looks too much like a gypsy to really be one. I will wager there is a well-bred *bint* under those tapestries."

Farid always mixed in some Arabic with whatever language he happened to be speaking. People often asked for a translation and got used to it, automatically translating words he used on a regular basis. It was not clear whether he was on a campaign to teach everyone a few words of Arabic or truly preferred the beautiful language. As he so often claimed in interminable discussions, sometimes keeping Carlo up until the first light of morning, Arabic was the most expressive of all medium forms of communication.

"Certain things just cannot be said in any language other than in this 'tongue of the angels,'" Farid was fond of saying.

His curiosity got the best of him, and eventually Carlo found his way to Carmelina's bed. He was surprised at how easily the conquest—at least in his mind a conquest—came about.

Afterward, laying prone on her bed, watching her draw her plump, tight lips on a cigarette, he whispered, "Carmelina, what are you? Are you the gypsy you pretend to be? Who are you really? Farid thinks you are an aristocrat under your disguise of a gypsy. Can that be true?"

"Ha!" she puffed out smoke. "You really want to know? What does it matter? No one ever really wants to know who we are underneath any of our disguises do they. Do we really want them to know? But I suppose it is only fair I tell you who I am since I already know who *you* are."

Carlo sat up jerkily, "You do? How do you know who I am? Who told you anything about me?"

She laughed, a sweet giggle of a laugh that said, "You silly little baby lamb."

"We know this train inside out, Carlo. It is our office after all," she said as if sharing a deep dark secret in confidence with him.

"Now you *must* tell me who you are," Carlo insisted laughing at what he thought was a joke.

"Should I?" she asked mysteriously.

Carlo held her bare upper arms and let his large hands caress the graceful muscles. He leaned over her and brought his face close to hers.

"Yes," he whispered, realizing he really did want to know everything about her.

She smiled and gently pushed him away.

"Very well then. I will tell you but you will probably not believe me. I was brought up just inside the Porta San Sebastiano," she said nonchalantly.

"What?" Carlo exclaimed. "You, you are Roman? I, I do not believe it."

"I told you that you would find it hard to believe, but it is quite true. It is also true that I used to teach school there. Of course, I do not spend much time in Rome anymore, but that is who I once was...."

Carlo silenced her lips with an affectionate kiss.

"Che bella, my beautiful Carmelina," he said affectionately realizing her mysterious past only made her more desirable.

He kept seeing her regularly after that. She was in the food he prepared and the wine he decanted. In the hotness of the stove and the coolness of the wash water; in the rumble-clack of the train and the river of steam it left behind, he was constantly aware of her presence in his life whether she was right there with him or not. He began to dream of what life would be like with her by his side.

Farid watched Carlo, shook his head and smiled—a smile that brightened two large white eyes on his brown face. Farid knew something Carlo did not. The dreams Carlo Maestoso savored were not true visions of the future he thought he would have with the beautiful Carmelina. Farid had seen too many men come through her life and knew she was on a mission of her own and it was not to end up with a lowly chef on the Orient Express.

"I suppose I should have warned you, my friend," Farid said. "But you seemed so happy, I did not have the heart to break your bubble ahead of time."

Carlo listened in sad silence. One day his beautiful Carmelina was beside him and the next she was not even on the train. The train was moving steadily eastward through Bulgaria, but Carmelina was on her way to her castle in the mountains.

Farid continued, "You do not know women, that is clear, but you are beginning to learn aren't you. What has just happened is a lesson you must remember from here on! So, the woman of your dreams has gone off with Monsieur LaTranche to his mansion in the mountains, so what? So what have you learned my young friend?"

"How could you know what she was going to do? How could you have not told me?" Carlo asked, still not believing she had left without even a good-bye.

"Ah, my Carlo. Would you have believed me even if I had told you? How could I know what a woman like her was going to do?" Farid leaned back and exhaled audibly. "The kicks and beatings of life teach us many things my young friend. That is how I could know. You are still young. I have been through it all. Do you know what women are, my friend?"

"What...what are they?" Carlo asked innocently.

"Ha! Despite being among God's most magnificent creations, they are"—Farid paused dramatically—"they are a distraction from the things that really matter."

"The things that really matter? What things are those things?" Carlo said sadly. "Carmelina really mattered to *me*."

"Yes, yes, of course she did," Farid smiled. "But I mean the things that will make a difference in your future like your work, your cultural development, your spirituality, your destiny, and the ultimate meaning of life, my young friend. It all boils down to God!"

"I stopped thinking about things like that a long time ago. I do not believe God really cares...," Carlo started to explain.

"You believe in the perfection of a special dish, don't you? You believe in pleasing a diner so much that he demands to meet you, right? You believe in life, right?"

"Of course, who does not?" asked Carlo totally confused at what Farid was trying to tell him.

"Well, how much life do any of us have left, I wonder," Farid finally said, obviously coming to the point. "Have you taken the time to notice what kind of shape the world is in today?"

"Okay, you just jumped from one subject to another. I have no idea what you are talking about, Farid," Carlo admitted realizing this conversation was not making him feel any better.

"Ha! Of course not. You have been far too busy with trivialities and chasing after false dreams. Believe me, my friend there are sounds in the air of bad things—a distant thunder is being heard just beyond the horizon," Farid shared ominously.

Farid said the last phrase in Arabic for added dramatic effect, but it was totally lost on his young friend.

"For heaven's sake, Farid, speak plainly and in a language I can understand," Carlo said getting annoyed at his friend's obviously lack of compassion for him after just losing the love of his life to another man.

"See how impoverished you are. You could have been learning Arabic from me all these months if you had not been so distracted by the pretty and seductive Carmelina," Farid admonished shaking his head at Carlo.

"Please Farid, I was in love," Carlo whined realizing just how foolish that sounded even to him right now.

"In love?" Farid laughed out loud, "You think you were in love? You cannot even bake a good baklava."

Carlo straightened up, a sternness in his face, "I *can* bake baklava!"

"You do not do it properly," Farid challenged him. "You use the wrong combination of nuts and sugars even though I have told you a hundred times."

"But what has this to do with anything?" exclaimed a now totally frustrated Carlo.

"Let me tell you, my inexperienced young friend," Farid said as he pulled up a chair and sat facing Carlo. "It seems to me there will be a great war and it is not too far off. I do not think this company will even be able to keep the Orient Express running much longer."

Farid paused for a moment, obviously wrestling with himself about how much more to tell his young friend. His sources had been feeding him some delicate information concerning activities in Germany that could be affecting the whole of the European community.

"I am going to leave the train at Istanbul, my friend, and make my way home to Damascus. Come with me. Yes, I want you to come with me," Farid said as if just making up his mind to invite his young friend to join him. "Damascus is the oldest city in the world, you know. It can teach you much about life. *I* can teach you much."

"Damascus, City of Paul," Carlo whispered as he remembered his religious training.

Carlo was more than stunned. He had done no thinking at all about the possibility of leaving his position. The Orient Express had become his home. He had thought his future was to be with Carmelina. Farid had been right about her. Could it be that what Farid was saying about the Orient Express was true as well? Would his home soon cease to exist? What of his dream of a life with Carmelina? If he left the train with Farid would he lose any chance of ever seeing her again? Was it indeed best to just forget the whole affair as Farid seemed to be suggesting?

"I...I can't," he said. "Not now, not yet."

"Very well, my friend. Think about it, though. Please promise me that much. Do it later, but do it. You know where to find me when you are ready. Come to Damascus, and soon. I fear the things that are coming are coming very quickly now."

Carlo and Farid exchanged a "ma' essalame, alla i sallmak"—"arrivederci, e tante belle cose" over glasses of misty raki in the cathedral-like-ceiling lounge of the Wagon-Lits Pera Palace Hotel in Istanbul. Farid was very much "his own Moslem," as he liked to put it, and had no problem with alcohol. He pretty much followed his own version of religion and service to his god.

"I am going to see if I can get on a ship to Beirut from here. What do you say, Carlo? Come with me to Damascus," Farid invited one more time, still hoping his young friend could put his affair with Carmelina behind him.

Carlo sipped his drink, "I do not know why, but I have decided I want to see Italy again first. I will join you, Farid. Just give me time to work it out my own way."

Carlo did not immediately put it together, but as he finished his drink, he did indeed know why he wanted to go to Italy first. Carmelina had said she had been brought up just inside the Porta San Sebastiano, just outside of Rome. He had to know for sure he would never see her again before he could move on with his life. He had not yet learned when to hold on and when to let go. That lesson would come soon enough. Sooner than he really wanted or dreamed as a matter of fact.

There was some time before the train left, so Carlo and Farid walked some of the streets of Istanbul. It was a city smelling of smoke, bridging Europe and Asia, never really making up its mind where it belonged. Farid proudly pointed out the magnificent blue-tiled mosque of Ahmet. They browsed through a bazaar filled with Turkish handicrafts, gazed at the Sea of Marmora, and listened to distant strains of a Janissary ensemble.

At Sikerci Station, they locked arms in a sustained farewell embrace. Carlo boarded the train, and as the Express slowly pulled out, he kept looking at Farid standing on the platform, a short figure waning in the distance, and he thought he heard the evening chant of a muezzin. He hoped he and his friend Farid would find what they were truly looking for in life.

The company had provided a young, relatively inexperienced helper as a replacement for Farid, so the entire responsibility for the cuisine on the return trip fell to Carlo. He even had to bake the baklava. Farid had been right. The passengers noticed the difference. They did not exactly complain, but they made it known it was a different-tasting baklava from the usual.

Carlo was also to experience a different taste well in the future. It would involve another delicacy made for another discerning taste. His osso buco, a dish he prepared especially for the pontiff, was to reveal a secret on a very important occasion in his not too distant future.

He managed to cable Carozza about his own resignation from Zagreb, and left the train at Venice on his way to Rome. It had become increasingly clear from reports received on the way that things were indeed beginning to boil in Europe. There were rumors of the line closing down proving his friend Farid had been right in his dire prediction of that as well. Perhaps he should have gone with Farid after all. Well, still time for that once he convinced himself once and for all that he had no future with the lovely and mysterious Carmelina.

Carlo took a last, solitary look at the dining car before he got off. This car had provided an elegant ambiance of his best work as a chef. The neatly place tablecloths, the fine silverware and china, the mini-menus upright in their holders at each table, marked with the golden arrow symbol of the Compagnie Internationale des Wagons Lits et des Grand Express Europeans. He could never have imagined that in just one short year, a car just like this would be the scene of the surrender of France to the Nazis. Another reminder that Farid had been justified in his return to his own country.

For now, though, Carol was a search of his own. As Carlo walked the long platform of the Venice station toward the motor launch-agitated waters of the Grand Canal, a mist gathered in his eyes. Carlo had some serious thinking to do, and Venice was a very conducive locale for that. The extraordinary silence of the city, despite the modern innovation of motor launches, gave rise to a calmness of spirit that was not like anything one finds anywhere else. Faint sounds floated over the narrow inner canals in the early morning hours. The voice of a matinal gondolier, the cry of a bird, the hollow chime of a church bell, and the never ceasing lap of the gentle sloshing of cool water.

Even as the day grows old and the vicos come alive with people, the containment of contemplation remains. The natives themselves are among the calmest of all people. The pace is slow. One walks, strolls or goes by boat from place to place in Venice. Speed finds no place among the people here. The stillness of a Venetian evening is totally incomprehensible. Even in the midst of the sounds of a festive crowd at one of the cafes in the Piazza, one knows that just beyond sleeps a quiet lagoon. This knowledge, this image of quiet and peace suffices to generate a constant restful joy. Venice was designed for meditation.

And meditate is what Carlo did. He took slow walks around the town, stopped frequently to enjoy some beautiful scene, and thought about his life. He was surprised at how much he missed Farid. He felt closer to him than anybody. He had hardly known his mother who had died when he was three. His father had died two years ago. And Carmelina...well, Carmelina had nearly killed him. Farid seemed his only friend. Should he go to Damascus? Surely he could find a ship here, a freighter perhaps, on which he could get passage, possibly as a cook. Should he investigate the possibilities? Questions, so many questions. How could he make any decision at all until he had some answers?

He stood on the bridge of the Academy one Sunday afternoon, drinking in the view of the sun-warmed Grand Canal. On his left, a red building with tiny terraces backed by rows of typical Venetian-style pointed arches grew out of the water, a cluster of red-and-white striped poles sprouting at its base where two launches were moored. Directly in front of him, two or three launches were quietly purring on the blue canal, which veered off to the left in the distance where he could clearly see the twin white domes of Santa Maria della Salute.

Around the bend continuing east, the canal would contact the tourist center of the city, the Riva degli Schiavone, Piazza S Marco, and then blend with the Canale della Giudecca at the magnificent S Giorgio Maggiore. Moving west, however, the Canal Grande curved its way through the middle of the city spawning scores of tributaries, those narrow waterways that sliced the city into an interconnected network. One could reach any part of Venice by traveling along the proper sequence of streams in this extensive web of water.

Carlo felt connected to the whole city. The water below him would touch the railway station, and well to the west, the lido, the island of Murano, in fact, the Adriatic, the Mediterranean, Athens, Beirut...Damascus. The world was one interconnected network. Perhaps the people in it were also.

Is it possible that as I stand here, I am somehow connected to Farid? Could it be that an action of mine will have an effect on his life, and vice-versa? Is there an underlying mystical network that relates all of us, each to the other? And what of God? Farid always talked about God. Is this invisible web I am thinking about God? Is there a purpose to the way we all fit together in our places? What thoughts! The daze of this place is making me crazy.

However, Carlo felt the need to talk to someone about these questions. His mind still misted with thoughts of interlacing canals, networks, and spiritual connections as he strolled to Santa Maria della Salute and had several cups of foaming espresso with a certain Padre Paolo. He left for a seminary in Rome a few weeks later. He was now on a path toward a future that he could never have dreamed of even in his wildest thoughts. He was on his way to a very important part in the destiny of more people than he had yet met in his short lifetime.

Chapter 5

The Osso Buco Fiasco

*Y*oung Sister Anna hurried into the Vatican's kitchen, a tremor in her slight figure.

"The old man, Father Carlo, is acting up again," she said to Sister Simione, the head cook of the Vatican.

"What is wrong this time?" asked Sister Simione, deciding the retired teacher needed something to do with his life other than trying to oversee her kitchen. "Wine not to his taste, perhaps?"

She slammed a large skillet down onto the stove and turned her huge bulk to face Sister Anna. Her hands were on her hips. She was frustrated but she must not take it out on the young Sister Anna.

"Well?" she said loudly, trying hard to regain her composure so as to not unduly frighten the novice nun.

"No," said Sister Anna meekly, always fearful when caught between these two opposing forces. "It is the osso buco. He demands to see *you* about it."

"Lord, give me patience," Sister Simione prayed. "What—"

The kitchen door crashed open as Father Carlo Maestoso burst in screaming, "What in the name of heaven are you people doing in this place? This is supposed to be a kitchen of some reputation."

He stood before Sister Simione like a bulldozer about to knock over a fence, "Since when do you make an osso buco like *that*?"

"Since the Holy Father told me that is the way he likes it," she said calmly.

"Bah! What nonsense! He would never tolerate such insipidity. Why it hardly has a hint of garlic," Carlo exclaimed as if every chef knew better. "When did he tell you this?"

"It was actually Signore Gianfredo, his valet who told me," Sister Simione admitted.

"Ah ha! That weasel," Carlo exclaimed as if that explained it all. "Then you did not speak to the Holy Father at all?"

"No," Sister Simione said sadly. "In fact, I have not seen him since he came back from his horrible trip."

"Nor have I," Carlo interrupted. "Don't you think, Sister Simione, that something strange is going on here? Since when has the pontiff's tastes in food changed so drastically?"

"I don't know. It was a horrifying trip for His Excellency, maybe his stomach—" Sister Simione said shaking her head.

"Well, I know! Something is not right. I do not like it," Carlo declared emphatically, "I don't like it one little bit and I will get to the bottom of this foolishness!"

He brushed past Sister Anna and left the kitchen in a huff. It was odd, too odd, and he was not one to let things go as they were. His many years as a teacher and scholar had taught him the value of thorough investigation and follow-up. He had been a demanding professor after seminary. Having been trained under strict authority, he aptly continued that style in his own teaching. Some people felt that even now, in his semi-retired status, he tended to act as though his authority were supreme whether in the classroom or the kitchen. Everyone knew of his expertise in both areas.

That dish was not to Pius' taste, indeed! Carlo had engaged in many a culinary discussion with his young friend when Pius was in the seminary. They had experienced together a variety of cuisines. Pius knew very well what osso buco should taste like. Carlo could not imagine Pius ordering it the way it had been prepared no matter how upset he was at the death of his friend. No, something was going on and was definitely connected to that trip. Something was not right and had not been right since the pontiff's quick return from the mountains.

Why was he being prevented from seeing the pontiff? Everyone on the staff knew how close they were. Now to find out that Sister Simione had also not had any personal contact with the pontiff since the trip merely added fuel to his fired up determination to get to the bottom of this. He would have to confront Gianfredo, the pontiff's personal valet, and make one more attempt to see his friend, Pius. He had his chance the next day when he spotted Gianfredo in a corridor. There was no one else around. All the better to try and get some answers from the pontiff's personal valet.

He went up to him and said in a booming voice, "I am going to need to see the Holy Father, immediately."

"I...I am sorry, Monsignor, but if you go up there, you will find a guard at the door," Gianfredo tried to explain.

"A guard?" exclaimed Carlo. "Since when is there a guard posted outside the pontiff's door?"

"His Holiness left strict orders not to be disturbed. Cardinal degli Alfieri sent the guard to insure the pontiff's privacy," Gianfredo told Carlo as if sharing an intimate secret with a fellow staff member.

Carlo was not about to accept that, especially now that he knew Domenico was involved somehow, "Degli Alfieri, eh?"

Carlo came close to Gianfranco, his huge paunch almost touching the other's body, forcing him back against the wall, "You go tell His Holiness that I wish to speak with him. He will see *me*!"

Gianfredo's nape was moist with perspiration as he stammered, "I...I am sorry, Monsignor, I cannot do that. The orders are—"

"To the devil with your orders," shouted Carlo as he stormed down the hall.

Later that day, after quiet, solitary meditation in the chapel of the Blessed Sacrament in the basilica to calm his anger and help him think straight, Carlo called his friend, the Minister of the Interior. Things were definitely not right and he knew just what he needed to do to unveil those involved in what looked more and more like a conspiracy, possibly against His Holiness himself. There was no way Pius would voluntarily sequester himself from even his closest friends especially after such a tragic accident in the mountains.

The next day, Carlo invited a hesitant Alfredo Gianfredo to his chambers to meet two young priests. He made Gianfredo sit down while he and his companions paced the floor. They did this in complete silence for a few moments. Gianfredo shifted uneasily, looking first to one person, then to another, suspicious this was more than a casual invitation from Father Carlo.

"Really, Monsignor," Gianfredo said trying to maintain some form of dignity, "I—"

"Silence," ordered Carlo, looking at him sternly. "Suppose I told you that I knew what you and degli Alfieri are up to, huh?"

Carlo was standing directly in front of Gianfredo, staring at his face. The priests were just behind him, one on each side. Carlo had indeed learned the lessons of discerning truth from lies just as his friend Farid had begun to teach him so long ago. Gianfredo's body language was definitely revealing a fear that his secret was no longer secure. His lips were trembling, his eyes were blinking rapidly, and they were darting to different parts of the room as if looking for an escape.

"What...what do you mean?" he stammered trying to maintain some form of composure though it was beginning to feel like a losing battle.

"You know perfectly well what I mean," Carlo boomed, a veritable cannon that echoed not only through the room, but in Gianfredo's head as if to decapitate him right there where he sat.

Gianfredo, sweating profusely by now, got up as if to run out of the room, "I...I must go immediately!"

In an instant, the other two priests were upon him, gripping him by the arms, one on either side. Gianfredo's face flushed red, indignant and frightened at the same time.

"What...what is this? Who are you? You have no right to detain me!" Gianfredo declared though it was becoming painfully clearly they had no intention of releasing his arms.

"Under the circumstances," said one of the priests, "we have *every* right. As officers of the Publica Sicurezza, we will put you under arrest on the spot if you do not tell Monsignor Maestoso what he wants to know."

"Sit down, you insect!" Carlo shouted. "Or I will fix it so they will not have anything to arrest!"

Gianfredo got back into the chair. The two detectives disguised as priests stood on either side of it to insure his complete cooperation.

"Now then," Carlo said. "Pius XIII is not here at the Vatican, is he?"

Gianfredo was silent. *How much could the old fool know?* he thought. *Surely Domenico had covered everything so there was no way Carlo could know anything for sure. The old man was merely bluffing, on a fishing expedition.*

"Well, is he?" Carlo demanded a second time.

Silence again. Gianfredo was sweating profusely, but had opted to remain silence so he would not inadvertently reveal something Carlo did not know. At this point he was beginning to wonder which would be worse, the wrath of Domenico or the threat of prison from Carlo. It was not an easy choice.

As if reading his mind, Carlo moved closer and bent over Gianfredo, his enormous frame bearing down on him.

"These detectives can put you away for quite a long time you know," he whispered close to Alfredo's ear. "Have you seen the inside of a Roman jail lately? It is really not a very pleasant place. Nothing like life here in the Vatican I assure you!"

"I...I..." stammered Alfredo, still hoping to figure out what Carlo did or did not know.

"Yes? Out with it you fool. What are you and degli Alfieri doing?" Carlo demanded sure now that a serious plot was in play.

Gianfredo whispered, "Degli Alfieri is only thinking about the betterment of the Church."

"Ha! About himself you mean," Carlo spit out in disgust. "The Church indeed. Don't you know what degli Alfieri is? That half-woman only thinks about his own perverse appetites! Now, you tell me the truth right now. I am asking you for the last time. The one who is here is not Pius XIII, right?"

Gianfredo closed his eyes and pressed his lips together tightly. He could have been praying, but they both know he was not. He was not going to get out of this one alive if he did not tell Carlo what he wanted to know. Obviously there was a hole in Domenico's air-tight plan. Carlo somehow knew Pius was not here in the Vatican.

"Right," he said in a voice so low it was barely audible.

"And where is Pius, then?" demanded Carlo in a voice so low and menacing he even surprised himself with the passion behind it.

"A—Avignon, but he is safe," Alfredo said haltingly, only interested in trying to save his own skin at this point.

"Ha! Whose lamed-brained idea was *that*!" Carlo asked.

"M—mine," Alfredo admitted.

"That figures. You idiot!" Carlo said with disgust. "Get this horrible excuse for a man out of here and see that he does not contact anyone but Domenico degli Alfieri concerning his unexpected need to leave the Vatican. Monitor his call and then escort him to his new quarters until we confirm the safety of the pontiff.

Later that day, Domenico degli Alfieri received a telephone call from Alfredo Gianfredo informing him that he was unexpectedly called away due to the death of his aunt in Caserta. He would be back, however, in time for the important papal audience next week.

With Gianfredo's information, which he had finally provided in detail, the Italian police had no trouble forming a plan to rescue the real pontiff from Avignon. Unifying the various competing forcers was another matter, however. Carlo pressed for the selection of the best men from the different divisions: the Sicurezza, the Carabinieri, the special prison detail, etc. Since the Minister of the Interior recognized the special urgency of the situation, a select group was organized in just two days.

At Avignon, the element of surprise was their greatest weapon. A minimal guard had been set on the Pope so it was a swift operation in which not a shot was fired, and no one was hurt. Interrogation of those who were in charge of guarding the Pope revealed that a telephone call was to be made by them to degli Alfieri every evening at eight o'clock. Only one word was to be said: "Gourbet." This was a signal that all was in order. The Minister himself wasted no time arranging for this to be continued.

Pius XIII had been in hiding in Castel San Angelo for three days now since his rescue from Avignon. Carlo had been ecstatic when he finally saw his friend face to face and that Pius was indeed in good health. Carlo and the police had then formulated a plan to intercept degli Alfieri's party on their way to the Piazza S. Pietro for the audience. In just one hour, the Vatican palace was to become a battlefield. However, none of those involved realized just how much of a blood bath it was about to become. There were those who had become part of this complicated web of deception that no one had even considered as players. One such player was Luciano's flirtatious "friend" Maria Penkova.

Chapter 6

Maria Penkova

*S*he stood in Piazza S. Pietro nervously awaiting the Pontiff's appearance, which was but thirty minutes away. Luciano had suddenly contacted her and told her where to stand in order to get the best view. She had not been able to communicate back with him, but had determined to be here in the Piazza as he had instructed. Her real hope was to see Luciano whose job it was to guard the pontiff. She had some very important "things" to show him.

"Right on this spot," he had said, "and you will not miss him."

Maria Penkova had arrived early and was beginning to feel a tension in her slender legs. The weight of the secret in her womb did not help either. There was another secret, too. It was in the backpack she was wearing, and it dominated her thoughts at the moment even more than the baby she carried within her.

Maria was only twenty-three, but she had lived a rough life for one so young. The first thing one noticed about her was the extraordinary moon-like roundness of her tanned face. Her eyes were large, dark, and also very round. Their shape was exaggerated by the chic, thick-rimmed, round glasses she wore. Her full red lips indicated a receptive softness, as though they would melt with the slightest pressure. Her hair was black, straight, and long enough to flow down over the top of the backpack. It carried the fragrance of a mixture of fresh blossoms. She always took great care with her grooming. It was, after all, very important to her "profession."

Strange, after all her seductions, conquests, exhilarating, but ultimately disappointing encounters, it was the first time she was experiencing the wonder of a life developing within her. She had begun to notice the swelling of her breasts several months ago, and when the regularity ceased, she was sure. There was no doubt in her mind that it was Luciano's baby, but now Luciano had abandoned her just like all the others. She had thought that perhaps in Luciano she had found what she had been searching for all her life. But the coward did not even tell her himself they were finished. Out of nowhere, this smooth-talking Cardinal degli Alfieri had called her and seemingly spoke for Luciano.

"Maria Penkova, please," he had said in what to her sounded like a snake like hiss.

"This is Maria Penkova," she answered tentatively, definitely not liking the sound of this man's voice.

"I am Cardinal degli Alfieri. You do not know me, but I am calling on behalf of my nephew, Luciano Steidler," the snake like voice hissed in her ear.

"Oh, Luciano. How is he?" Maria said without thinking. "I have been anxiously waiting to hear from him. Is anything wrong?"

"No, no, no. Nothing is wrong, my daughter," Cardinal degli Alfieri said smoothly, "In fact, he is in the best of health and spirits, I assure you."

"But, then, why—"

"He has been greatly honored by the Holy Father with a special assignment which will take him away for a while," Cardinal degli Alfieri told her.

Away for a while, Maria thought. She knew what that meant. "Then…I will not be seeing him again?"

"Not for a while," Cardinal degli Alfieri answered her, careful not to make it sound permanent, though he knew it would be. "He sends all of his love and will be in touch with you as soon as he can."

Her anger flared as she hung up the phone. What was it she wanted from Luciano or any man for that matter? To stay with them? More likely to use them. Use them for what? These were the questions that had plagued her all of her life. From the very beginning it seemed, starting with the first man she ever knew, her father, she had been haunted by this necessity to strive, compete, and overcome. Her father. The very thought of him was enough to bring the taste of bile to her mouth and a gnawing rot in her stomach.

There were three older brothers in her family. There had also been a baby sister, little Sophia, who never got a chance to live a full life. The Penkovs lived in Varna, and Maria's father worked as a mechanic, plumber, and general handyman at the nearby complex of resort hotels in Drujba on the Black Sea. This was a sprawling patch of acreage several hundred feet back from the beach. Lusciously landscaped with grassy hills and an abundance of shade trees, it had been energetically developed by the Bulgarian government as a prime tourist attraction.

The buildings had been constructed mainly by Swedish concerns, and were ultra-modern in facilities as well as design. The center of the entire layout was the Grand Hotel Varna, a high-rise, sparkling white, rectangular structure. The dreamlike city contrasted sharply with the actual town that sat just on the outskirts, well out of view of the rich tourists the resort hoped to attract. The town where the majority of the workers came in from to work at the resort was a poor, unkempt village that reflected the basic rural nature of the country as a whole.

The tragedy for the Pankov family happened on what should have been a happy holiday. It was Maria's tenth birthday, and her father, Blago Pankov had taken the day off from his work. He was taking his family on a tour of Drujba, the hotels, the shops, the scenic walks, and of course, the beautiful beach. They had just realized that the three year old was missing when the commotion broke out behind them. People were hurrying across the sand towards the water.

"I think somebody drowned," a little boy shouted as he ran passed them toward the beach.

In a few moments, a muscular young man was carrying Sophia's lifeless little body away from the shore in search of the child's parents.

Maria's mother screamed and fainted when she saw the lifeless body of her youngest daughter. Maria herself was frightened and confused. The impact of it all did not hit her until several days later.

"You are my only jewel now, Maria," her father had said at the funeral. "My only jewel. I must guard you, keep you under lock and key. Nothing must happen to you!"

The Penkovs were one of the few Roman Catholic families in the area, and a funeral mass was said. The priests tried their best to help the church family through their time of grief, but consolation was impossible. The church wept uncontrollably at the untimely death of one of their youngest members. Neighbors remarked about how incredible it was that Maria's mother got through it all with seemingly unnatural strength. The truth was she had entered a trance-like state ever since she had viewed the body of her dead daughter. It seemed to Maria that she never completely came out of it from that day on ever again.

Blago, understandably, began to assume a more active role in family matters. To the boys he gave considerable freedom, but Maria was forbidden almost everything. She was hardly ever left alone. Bed and bath became her only occasions for private thoughts and explorations. She was the only female in this world, and she had to learn about herself, by herself. Her mother was not only not available but even if Maria was allowed near her, she was totally uncommunicative.

She tried, to the extent she was allowed, to be involved in her brothers' activities. These occasions were few and far between until just after her fourteenth birthday. One day Blago agreed to let her join the boys for a hike through some of the nearby hills. She was excited to finally be allowed out of her prison to explore some of the world around her home. Her father had entrusted her to the care of her brothers who were less than enthusiastic about their sister tagging along.

"Come on, Maria! You are so slow," they shouted as they ran ahead of her.

"You are holding us up," they chided her when it was obvious her physical stamina was sorely lacking.

She struggled, but the pain in her legs and the strain on her body caused her to stop frequently. The harder she tried, it seemed, the farther away they got from her. She kept hearing their voices, taunting her, and laughing. When she came to a small clearing, she fell to the ground. She sat there, cross-legged, motionless, and pensive waiting for them to find her on their way back. There was no way her body could endure this sudden burst of exercise.

It was at this time, as she sat exhausted, staring at the woods, that she saw herself in her father's arms. She was not sure is she was dreaming or having some kind of vision brought on by her physical exhaustion. She saw herself being carried by her father as though she were an infant. He took her to the top of the hill. When they reached the summit, he held her up high—shoulder height—and she could see a great, level expanse of what appeared to be a field of grain moving in the breeze like ocean waves. But it was not grain, it was a sea of people. People had crowded into a great square. They were waiting to see the Holy Father, her father told her. So many times her father told her about this man they all called the Holy Father. So many times had her father guided her behavior with the admonition, "The Holy Father would not like that." So often had Maria heard this phrase from his lips that this man seemed bigger than life itself with a power beyond even that of her father who had virtually kept her prisoner in her own home.

Then the picture in her vision changed. She was with her oldest brother. He was on his back on the ground and she was on top of him, beating him, or was he beating her? It was not really like a beating, no, instead it was very pleasant. He was not beating her, and yet she was not sure exactly what was going on. She looked at his face carefully as she lay on him and realized it was no longer the face of her brother, now it was the face of Sasho, one of her classmates. She felt her legs stretch and her body widen as she leaned hard on him. She felt pressure, then discomfort, followed by striving, tension, motion, tension, moistness—and a release that convulsed the universe in her body and her mind.

The jolting of the impact of her vision awakened her. She shook her head and looked around. She looked at the thick cluster of trees, but she did not see anyone. She cast her smarting eyes down to the damp earth, but she did not see it. It took a few moments for her to overcome this feeling of not knowing where she was. Then she remembered and felt a surge of joy, a satisfaction she had never before experienced as she relived the final moments of her vision.

It did not matter anymore that she could not keep up with her brothers. It did not matter much what her father would say to her. Nothing seemed to matter that much anymore. Tomorrow, she would look for Sasho. The vision had shown her how to bring not only satisfaction but even pleasure into her world.

She found Sasho a very willing partner when she approached him and explained her vision. They managed to meet on several occasions on a quiet stretch of beach or in the woods. Once they even had an opportunity to be together in his own bedroom.

"Again, Sasho," she pleaded, her arms around his neck. "Please, again."

Sasho obliged. She widened her young mouth in a delicious smile. He brought his lips to hers, and she embraced him with a pressure that startled him. But he held firm, and they climaxed. Maria lay quietly on her back for a few moments. She turned to Sasho and brought her face very close to his.

"Once more," she whispered.

Sasho was exhausted and drained. He hardly moved. She slapped him lightly on the cheek.

"Come on, Sasho. Just once more," she said pleaded learning already how to manipulate a man to get what she wanted.

He reached out and pulled her to him. She smiled as she realized the power she had over Sasho. It was time for her to see if it worked with others. It was not long before Maria stopped seeing Sasho, and went on to other partners. Her early teens were filled with clandestine sexual explorations, alone and with others. She could never rest. Even while she was with one partner, she would be planning the next exciting encounter. She was ever on the lookout for a new conquest. Her passion and search for excitement seemed insatiable.

In the meantime her father, Blago Penkov, was carrying around two clouds in his brain. Clouds that became darker and larger as time went on. One was a cloud of frustration and depression brought about by his wife's condition. He was an energetic man, and they had not been intimate in years. He had been throwing himself into his work, but that no longer satisfied him. Every time he saw a woman—any woman—his mind would move immediately in just one direction. He felt the softness of her breasts, the smoothness of her legs, his lips moistly pressing hers, his fingers slowly caressing....

He dreaded having to work on the beach. The nubile, gracefully figured tourists in their scant costumes set his brain ablaze. He often ended the day in a state of shameful remorse after inducing relief in the privacy of a public convenience. This was not Blago's way. Neither was whoring or unfaithfulness his way yet the cloud would not leave him.

He could not help noticing even his own daughter. This was the other cloud. He had watched her mature over the years, and realized that she was moving steadily further and further away from him. She had become a beautiful young woman. Woman? This was the real cloud. The cloud of doubt and fear. He quivered at the very thought of his precious jewel talking to young men, and of his precious jewel in their arms and in their beds. It was monstrous to even consider such a thing!

The clouds burst into a violent thunderstorm soon after Maria's eighteenth birthday. He had been ordered to check the air conditioning on the third floor of the Grand Hotel Varna. When Blago got out of the elevator, he stepped into a furnace. He had to get to the source of the trouble as soon as possible. It was a stifling, unbearable heat that threatened to suffocate all who entered the floor.

He noticed a young couple walking down the hall away from the elevator, their arms around each other's waists. The cooling unit was in the opposite direction, but as he walked away, the picture of the couple remained in his mind. The man had a full head of blond hair, and the girl's hair was long, black, and straight. Her attire and figure looked vaguely familiar.

Suddenly, his blood rushed to his temples and set them wildly pulsating as he suddenly realized the truth. He turned swiftly and charged down the hall like a demon out of the flames of hell. As the couple entered a room a few doors away, his heavy feet pressed the cushioned rug as his large frame moved forward faster than he had ever thought his huge body could move. His face was soaked in hot moisture, and his palms and forearms bathed in sweat. He rammed a pass-key into the lock and burst through the door.

"You filthy…," he roared as he grasped the man by the arm, pulled him from Maria, and threw him out of the room.

He shut the door and advanced toward his daughter. She screamed. His head was a mass of perspiration, his eyes blurred and red. He caught her by the arms and shook her violently.

"Papa! Papa!" she screamed in pain and terror.

He pushed her onto the bed and fell onto her. She pressed up against him, screaming.

"Papa! Papa!" she screamed over and over.

He held her immobile with a grip of steel. His lips found her ripe breasts, and he pressed on hard, taking in more and more through her sheer, braless blouse.

She kicked up her legs, trying to struggle away. Blago spun around and at the sight of the young naked flesh beneath the clothing. He was being driven crazy as the cloud in his brain burst into a roaring storm of pent up emotions. He grasped her thigh with his right hand. Writhing violently, she managed to slide free and run out of the room, gagging in tears of fright.

Blago was left on the bed, trying desperately to catch his breath as the slam of the door rang in his ears. A bright, deep red smear on his fingers told him he had done some serious damage to his beautiful jewel. He prayed he would die on the spot!

Maria never went home again. She had time to think while riding on a train to Sophia, and she began to understand, she thought, for the first time perhaps. This was the world of men, and these were the men of the world. All that loving protection from her father, all the caresses, all the talk of "his jewel, his precious," what was it all for? To save her for himself?

She began to shiver, and her stomach fluttered spasmodically, an unmistakable sensation at the back of her throat. She jumped up from her seat and walked quickly to a wash room at the end of the parking area. She locked herself in, and the moment she bowed her head over the basin, a stream of brown liquid gushed out of her mouth. She cried out, and tears ran down her cheeks. She screamed again as more fluid issued from her uncontrollably.

Somehow, despite the pain, the burning, and the sadness there was a spark of joy. It was as though she had spewed out all of her past, cleared away the ruins, and was ready to get in the game of life once again. But the memory of her father's act persisted. Her father must not be allowed to remain. Her father, who had betrayed her when she needed him, must be eliminated once and for all.

"Papa," she vowed even as she strove to remove herself from his influence, "I will avenge myself!"

When she returned to her seat on the train, she actually felt refreshed. She began to look out at the Bulgarian countryside gliding past. The rustic simplicity fit her mood. The multitude of mineral springs spoke to her of the refreshing she was suddenly feeling, and then the roses. There were fields and fields of them. The spectacular Damask roses waiting to be plucked in order to live again in the famous perfume. Maria smiled, her wide mouth lending a lovely glow to her face. She asked a porter for pen and paper, and began to scratch down some words. She thought as she stared out of the window into the distance. She wrote and then crossed things out. She jumbled words, rearranged phrases, inserted, and deleted them until finally she settled on a satisfactory version of what would be the first of her many poems.

Blossom
by
Maria Penkova

To think that a year has passed
A turn ago, I saw you last.

Nay, not you. A parent,
Appearing much the same.
Oh sweet burst of softness
What, do tell me, is your name?

It is life, it is love,
It is heaven, it is earth.
Blessed this bush
That gave you birth.

Let me love you while I may
For I know you cannot stay.

Day and dark,
Clouds and rain

Your beauty dies
I'm left in pain.

But be time granted
Then one day mild
My happy glance
Will find your child.

This was something new, and something wonderful. She would create more of it. She was certain of that. Strange, that although she had enjoyed poetry in school especially the limited but haunting work of Dimche Debelyanov, she never considered it as a means of expressing herself. At any rate, it certainly would not be her livelihood. She knew full well how she would support herself. An attractive young woman of her proclivities would never lack for money, of that she was very sure!

In fact, she had already noticed a middle-aged man at the Varna station who was apparently by himself on the train. In a matter of an hour or so, she had him engaged first in conversation and then in what was to become her "business." He was the beginning of a stream that never ceased flowing even after she met Luciano.

Maria had been in Italy for about a month when she first saw him. She was not sure what brought her here, but she knew somehow this was right where she needed to be, almost as though she were driven by some secret force—a mission, an assignment. She did not know, and she never thought about it in such clear terms, but she definitely felt she was being drawn by an unseen force. She made her way to Rome, and knew this was her place. Her purpose was to become clearer as the days went by and she became better acquainted with some of the characters of the netherworld in which she moved. Although she had continued to operate independently as an "Angel of Pleasure," as some Italians called it, she could not help but have contact with corrupt police, gamblers, pimps, black marketers, and terrorists.

On the periphery of all this, in another world, it seemed to her, was handsome Luciano. It was strange for her to have approached a Swiss Guard like that. It was the challenge, perhaps, or maybe the novelty of joining up with a soldier. She did not know what, but approach him she did. Dressed in blue shorts with a delicate white streak down the sides, a white top, shoulder-strap bag, and carrying a camera, she looked quite the typical tourist.

"Signor' guardia, may I take your picture?" she asked him, her round mouth open in an irresistible smile.

"Yes, of course," Luciano answered, at first hardly noticing her.

Maria aimed the camera, sighted, bent her knees ever so slightly, and snapped.

"Grazie," she said softly. "I will show it to you tomorrow."

She turned quickly, and walked away slowly. Luciano watched her, drinking in every movement—undulating fundament, rhythmic hips, and the bag that gently stroked her brown thigh with each calculated step.

Strange, of the hundreds of tourists who had photographed him, he never remembered any of them saying they would show him the picture. Would she really come back tomorrow? Why did he even care? Women. They barely interested him, and yet this one somehow seemed different. Why, he wondered, would this one catch his eye?

Maria did return the next day.

"I have something else for you," she said after showing him the picture.

"Oh?" he said smiling, surprised how pleased he was that she had returned.

"Yes," she said and handed him a folded sheet of paper.

He unfolded it and read.

Picture
by
Maria Penkova

Before the massive portal wide
A guardian of the land,
And all the ritual you abide.

Reflecting rainbows, still you stand
Watchful eyes, deep and blue
Stately stance and steady hand.

Hair of gold, tossed askew
A scabbard at your side,
This is my image here of you.

"So, you write verses," he said, looking down at her upturned face. "And in terza rima, too. Very nice."

"Ah. I see you know poetry. Do you write also?" she asked coyly, seeing that this man was even more intriguing than she had first thought.

"What Italian does not recognize Dante's verse form?" Luciano replied. "No, I do not write, but I love to read good poetry."

"This is a rather special terza rima, you know," she said as she smiled up at him. "Take another look at it."

Luciano studied the poem for a moment and then smiled.

"Ah, yes. I see," he said figuring out her puzzle. "Do you like to go around in circles?"

Maria smiled, and looked at him coquettishly, "That depends on the circles."

Luciano took the plunge. No one was more surprised than he.

"My circles perhaps?" he asked.

They met that night in Luciano's apartment and read from Gabriela Mistral's "Desolacion" and "Tala." They sat next to each other, reading aloud; sometimes only Luciano, sometimes Maria, sometimes in unison. They read slowly, musically, listening to each other's voices. Sometimes they paused and looked at each other. Moment by moment, Luciano felt drawn into her, her chime-like sound, her soothing glow, her rousing fragrance. Another pause, and they read no further that night.

For Luciano, it was all wonderment. One by one, Maria revealed her secrets, those of the lips, of the mamae, and the femurs. He had never been with a woman before. When she unveiled her last secret, his wonderment was complete. Scented softness, moist engulfment, waves of pleasure, and then an ocean of joy. They saw each other regularly after that. Though Maria really did enjoy her Luciano, she did not—indeed, could not—neglect the others. Her finances and her insatiable appetite would not allow her to be confined to only one relationship.

In particular recently, she spent much time with the man everyone called "Il Turco." Nobody seemed to know why he was called that, but it was a name that had stuck with him for many years now. Actually, he was part Greek, part Sicilian, and one of the leading suppliers of illegal armaments in Rome. He dealt with assassins, thieves, terrorists, and the like.

Maria knew all of this but was unexplainably fascinated by this man. Something, some buried compulsion, drew her to him. His appearance belied his trade, however, another mysterious factor about the man that continued to draw Maria to him. Groomed with the perfection of an actor about to go on stage, he paced the piazzas in the evenings with a neatly pressed jacket draped over his shoulders. He was never out during the day, and no one ever saw him without a lighted cigarette between the thumb and index finger of his left hand. It was always a Pharaoh, an expensive Egyptian brand not readily available on the streets.

Some said that his right hand was kept free to draw, at an instant's notice, the automatic pistol hidden under the jacket in a shoulder holster. His complexion was brown, but carried that characteristic Greek tinge of green. His eyebrows were dark and heavy, and he wore a razor-trimmed hairline moustache. He was actually quite a strikingly handsome man.

He showed Maria a selection from his arsenal one night that included a selection of automatics and revolvers both German and Italian. Then seeing her interest, he moved on to the American rifles and machine guns, grenades, and explosives. The ornate Japanese daggers really drew her interest, but it was one rather strange-looking piece which Maria actually asked about.

"Ah!" Il Turco said. "You have interesting taste, mia cara. That is a diabolical instrument."

Maria stared at the weapon, "What is it called?"

"It was developed by the British. Two fellows actually, Sheppard and Turpin, who were inventors," he explained. "Now, take the *S* from Sheppard, the *T* from Turpin, and the *EN* from England, and you get, STEN. It is called a Sten gun."

"Interesting. Why diabolical?" she asked totally intrigued by the deadly looking weapon.

"Ha! How many reasons do you want?" he quipped. "It is a favorite among terrorists; readily available, easily concealed, a hand-held machine gun capable of spraying death at the rate of five-hundred fifty rounds per minute. Here!"

He picked up the gun and handed it to her. She instinctively backed away though she was irresistibly drawn to the evil looking weapon.

"You can hold it," he said. "It is not loaded, and it only weighs about three and a half kilos. That is another nice thing about it. Even a slight beautiful woman like yourself could easily handle it though it packs a deadly power when discharged into the enemy."

Il Turco showed her how to hold it. Maria felt a sudden weakness in her legs. A tremor took hold of her, but it was a tremor of excitement as well as fear. Yes, this horrible thing excited her.

"How about ammunition?" she said, not understanding why she should ask such a question.

"Also readily available," he assured her, liking the interest she was showing in one of his favorite weapons.

"From you?" she asked, again surprising herself as well as Il Turco at her continued interest.

"But of course…What is it, my sweet? Are you planning a raid? Want to do some knee-capping perhaps?" he laughed, "Whatever it is, you will not miss with that thing, believe me."

"You—you pig!" she said as she laughed along with him.

"Ah, ah, ah," he said, waving a bony index finger. "I can see it is time for bed. Look, I know you are interested in this fine specimen of a weapon. I will let you have it cheap. Two nights ought to do it. One for the gun, one for the bullets. Okay?"

"Why do I stay with you?" Maria said, the hint of a smile on her lips. "I will think about it."

Maria could not sleep that night after she left Il Turco and returned to her own apartment in EUR. She reached for her eyeglasses and her watch on a table next to her bed. She saw it was a little after three in the morning. She got up, slowly made her way into the kitchen, and turned on the light. Her eyes registered a slight discomfort at the sudden brightness. She poured some Scotch 84 into a small glass, lit up one of Il Turco's cigarettes, took a pad and pen from a shelf, and began to write.

The words came swiftly, automatically, almost as though someone else were writing for her. She made only two corrections.

The Interior
by
Maria Penkova

From whence this cave that hides my heart?
This darkness I cannot dissolve.
Shadows, shadows of shadows, crushing
My soul.

In the deep winter of time we buried this,
But it springs again to have its vengeance.
I am constrained, compelled. There is no halt
To the pulse of death, the clan of Seth.

How very strange, she thought, after re-reading the poem several times. Frightening, but at the same time, satisfying. She did not know what to make of it, where it came from.

She was thinking about that poem now as the time for the Pope's appearance was just minutes away. She was very tired, and the heat had drained her physically. She lifted the straps of the backpack off her shoulders and swung the load onto the ground right in front of her feet. That was better, much better, but not only because she was tired. The heat and the exertion of carrying both the backpack, her child, and her deadly secret was beginning to once again bring visions back into her troubled brain. Soon, she told herself, soon it would all be complete!

Chapter 7

Audience

omenico degli Alfieri could hardly believe that the actual moment had finally arrived. Luciano looked wonderful. Everything was in order. He had been receiving the reassuring "Gourbet" every evening at the precise hour. He had taken every extra precaution he could think of in view of Maestoso's disturbing note. Yes, it would go well in spite of the foolish note. There was absolutely no way the old fool Maestoso could know anything of value much less interfere in any way. All was perfectly in place just as it should. It was the Lord's will acting through him. He was sure of it.

Where was Gianfredo? He was supposed to be back by now. Domenico had tried to reach him by phone several times, but could not. That man! He never really was reliable. A clown; he reminded him of his father. Odd that his father should come to his mind at this moment. His father, who was fond of performing macchiette—those humorous, one-man skits—at family gatherings. The audience would laugh in the beginning, and then end up in tears as his father concluded his performance. Typical Neapolitan mystique.

All foolishness he had thought then and even more so now. His father had been a fool. There was never any real purpose to anything he had ever done. No matter, his mother had seen to it that Domenico had received the education and refinement he craved, and now here he was, on the verge of his greatest victory. His mother would be incredibly proud of him, he was absolutely sure of it.

In any case, everything was set. He did not need Gianfredo anyway. The very minute was at hand. They would march out to the private Courtyard of St. Damascus adjacent to the Palace, and from there out of the Vatican grounds, through the bronze gate to Piazza S. Pietro where Luciano would be carried to the main entrance of the Basilica. He had a strong, faithful, and more than sufficient guard providing protection during the entire audience.

He made a last minute check with Luciano.

"You have your address all ready?" he asked.

Luciano smiled weakly.

"How many times have we gone over that?" Luciano chided him, then softened his voice. "Everything is under control. I am not worried."

Indeed, Domenico thought, *he should not be. He does not know about Maestoso's note, nor I do not want him to. No matter, I have taken care of everything! I have left nothing to chance! My plan is perfect! Absolutely perfect!*

"It is just that it is so important," Domenico said. "Today will begin a turnaround for the entire Church...and it is in your hands."

Luciano nodded agreeing with Domenico for the hundredth time it seemed. Finally, it was time to leave. Domenico directed the procession out to the courtyard. They were safely on their way. Nothing could stop them now!

Outside, Captain Rocco Baldossari had been appointed as the special officer in charge of the operation of deposing the false pope. He had been chosen because of his intelligence and experience, as well as for his physical prowess. Rocco was one of those men you did not want to run into on a dark street. The key word for describing him was *broad*. He was broad all over, one of the biggest men in any of Italy's police forces. He had been quite a successful wrestler in his younger days. He and his hand-chosen detachment were all dressed as Swiss Guards as they led Pius XIII through the passetto. Contrary to Rocco's wishes, Maestoso was also with them.

The passetto was a narrow, fortified passageway, built inside of a wall, which ran along the side of the street called Borgo S. Angelo. It led from Castel Sant'Angelo into the Via dei Corridori right through to the Papal Palace. It had been built many centuries ago as an escape route, and in fact, was so used by Clement VII during the sack of Rome in the early 1500s.

Baldossari had tried to convince Maestoso to remain behind in the castle because a violent encounter was anticipated once the two opposing factors engaged one another in the courtyard.

"Nonsense," Carlo cried. "I can be a useful guide for you. I know the ins and outs of the Vatican much better than you or any of your men. I insist on going with you."

Pius smiled and said, "Believe me, Captain Rocco, it is hopeless. Once he makes up his mind, only the direct intervention of Heaven will change it. I do not like it either, but the moment grows near. Let him come."

"It is as Your Holiness wishes—the matter is closed," Rocco said.

Domenico and his party were about halfway across the Courtyard of St. Damascus when Baldossari and his troops burst in behind them.

"Company...Forward!" Rocco shouted, his voice a raspy trumpet of impeding judgment.

The police split ranks, half going to the left and half to the right of the courtyard. Moving quickly, they soon had degli Alfieri's group trapped between them. They charged from both sides and prevented them from moving forward or backward.

Blades flashed, clubs found their targets, writhing bodies locked in struggles, some fell to the ground, and rolled on the pavement until one no longer moved. The courtyard reverberated with the noise of clashing steel, shouts, and thuds of pummeled flesh. Many received fatal wounds in those first few moments of the battle. Those outside could hear the noise of the approaching procession but had yet to see anything or perceive what was actually happening in the courtyard.

Domenico, attempting to help Luciano hold his position, was pushed violently into a column and knocked senseless. Just before he lost consciousness, he saw the white-robed figure, surrounded by Swiss Guards, being led out the other end of the courtyard. We had won were his final thoughts and then he was forced to close his eyes as the blackness overtook him!

At the same time, Carlo, guiding Pius XIII forward toward the center of the courtyard, received a club-thrust in the stomach that sent him to the ground moaning. He was following Baldossari, who was beating a path through, until four men pounced on him and finally halted his progress.

Carlo was in a delirium of pain. Through his mist-veiled eyes, he managed to see the Pontiff being led by his guard out the other end of the courtyard. It was over. They had accomplished their mission. Blessed be the Lord he thought as he, too, sank into darkness.

The crowd in Piazza S. Pietro had swelled to near capacity by the time the Pope was being carried out, high above the throngs, on the sedila. Bodies were pressed against bodies. Maria felt closeness on all sides, and this added to her discomfort from the heat. She was very close to the main entrance of the Basilica through which the pope was to be carried.

The people began to cry out and applaud. There were citizens of many nations. Italians, Greeks, Germans, Spaniards, Arabs, Americans, Englishmen, and Irish all mixed together, and their cry was as one.

"Viva Il Papa! Viva Il Papa!"

Maria watched the pontiff's progress across the square very closely. The white robed figure, the tiara bobbing gently over the heads of the crowd, which gradually became larger and more distinct. He extended his arms in a gesture of peace. He blessed the people, and they roared in response.

"Viva Il Papa!" they said in unison.

It rang out from everywhere. The air itself was electrified with its energy.

Suddenly Maria saw the ocean of grain waving before her while cradled in her father's arms. It was the vision she had seen while waiting in the woods that day for her brothers to find her and bring her back home. She knew what she had to do. Her mission had never been clearer. The vision had prepared her for this very day!

"Viva Il Papa!" the crowd roared.

The pope was very close to her now. The grain became a crowd of people once again, but her mission was still so ingrained in her brain that it mattered not if they were people of waves of grain. The end result had to be the same. She must avenge herself!

"Viva Il Papa!" they shouted, louder and louder until it totally overwhelmed her senses.

The heat was suffocating her. Maria felt that her very pores were stifled. Her hands were soaked, her legs in pain, and her back covered with moisture. She saw the grain again and it reenergized her once again.

"Viva Il Papa!" rang out from the grain over and over again.

"Il Papa!" someone shouted very loudly right next to her ear.

He was practically next to her.

"Papa!" she shouted. "Papa!"

With the swiftness of a cobra she reached into the backpack on the ground in front of her, and tightened her grip on cold steel.

"Viva Il Papa! Il Papa! Papa!... Papa!"

A hot, exploding shower of death engulfed the pontiff. Bright red blotches smeared the blazing white robe. Immediately, a heavy cover was thrown over him as he sank down nearly out of sight.

Maria heard a woman's voice screaming, then she realized it was her own voice. Her voice continued screaming as three guards pinned her to the ground. She screamed as she saw the face of her father. Then she clearly saw another face.

"Luciano! It was Luciano!" she cried. "Luciano!"

Her father's bulk was once again hovering over her. She had to kill him. She had to kill Papa.

"Was he dead?" she screamed though it appeared no one could understand or even hear her.

Someone yelled, "The Holy Father has been shot. He is dead!"

She had done it. She had accomplished her mission. She could rest now. Her work was done. She slipped into oblivion.

Yes, her mission was done, but not as she had envisioned it. Maria Penkova would not live long enough to realize just exactly what she had done, though she did deliver her child though quite prematurely.

Conclusion

t was almost two weeks after the horrible incident, and Domenico degli Alfieri was confined to quarters. He had been unconscious for many days after the severe blow to the head he received in the courtyard. A police guard was stationed in front of his office-apartment, and food was brought in to him. Whenever he expressed the desire to celebrate Mass, he would be escorted by two guards to a convenient chapel, then escorted back.

It had taken him a few days to realize he was under house arrest. He had no recollection of how he had gotten back to his quarters. He did not understand why he was in this predicament. The scene in the courtyard was still a blurred dream. Only now was some memory beginning to return.

Newspaper and television reports had informed him that the Holy Father was recovering from his wounds and would soon be back at work. But Domenico was uncertain who was recovering. Was it Luciano? Was it Pius? He dared not ask anyone. What he remembered was they had subdued Maestoso's henchmen before they had left the courtyard, hadn't they? Of course they had. Pius was out of the picture. But where was he?

As he tried to clear his mind and review the events that led up to the court-yard battle, he was sure there was no way Pius could have been there that day. He had received the code word signal that all was well at Avignon. No one knew where Pius was except his childhood friend, Alfredo Gianfredo.

Wait, Alfredo had not shown up the day of the audience. He had called two days before saying he had been called out of town because of a death in the family. Had he called to see if there was a record of a death in Alfredo's family?

Could Maestoso have gotten to Alfredo? Is that what the strange note from Maestoso meant? How could he have missed such an obvious breech in his brilliant plan?

Soon after Domenico had lunch, a young priest arrived with a sealed envelope from Carlo Maestoso addressed to him. He opened it at once curious to know once and for all what had really happened since the day of the audience.

11 June, 1942

Carissimo Domenico,

These idiotic medical men are still keeping me in a hospital bed. They claim I need more time to recover despite the fact that I feel quite well at this point.

But perhaps I should not complain. Their insistence has granted me a lot of time. I have used the time to go over in my mind the strange events that have transpired in the last few weeks. In addition, I have had a chance to read the very thorough reports of the deep investigation the police have made of the entire business concerning an insidious plot to install a bogus pope in office right under our noses. I have pieced things together, and I feel I need to share my thoughts and conclusions with you.

We know, of course, of the switch made during the vacation you arranged for Pius to take to the mountains. By the way, Doctor Enrico Lucreto has been replaced as well as the papal valet, Alfredo Gianfredo. All others who were part of this will be duly dealt with and punished for their part in the intended deception. Had it not been for the requested change in his menu, more specifically the osso bucco, Luciano might have been able to fool most of the staff, at least until after the audience which seems to have been your plan. What did you think would happen after that I wonder? What would have become of Luciano? It really is of no consequence now anyway is it?

Anyway, you must still have many questions as to what transpired in the courtyard and beyond that fateful day. It is difficult to decide where to begin. Perhaps at the center of the violence—Maria Penkova. From what I have learned of her unfortunate background, there would have been no preventing her action. Her sick mind drove her to it. No one was aware of it, and no amount of precaution could have stopped her. The Lord in His wisdom has seen fit to call this poor demented creature, who could not even be held responsible for her actions, to carry out His work. But her child survived the courtyard violence.

Maria regained consciousness only once, after the girl was born. They even let her see the baby. She seemed oddly at peace after weeks of what seemed to be a tormented coma. In a weak, barely audible voice, she said that she wanted to call her child Luciana, the Poet's "soul of light." The child has been so baptized and will be cared for by an appropriate agency. We must pray for the repose of Maria Penkova's tortured soul and for her now orphaned daughter.

Given the premise, then, that the assassination attempt had to take place, you, my dear Domenico, were the one responsible for allowing Pius XIII to continue his reign. It was your ill-conceived scheme that the Lord twisted in accordance with His will and used as protection for His true vicar.

Yes, Pius will soon be back, as the news reports are saying. However, contrary to the news reports he is recovering only from bruises suffered during the commotion in the courtyard prior to what is now being referred to as the assassination attempt.

Luciano, on the other hand, was killed. There was no helping him. His body, so terribly mangled by scores of bullets, that he was beyond any medical help. His death has been recorded as killed in the line of duty. The report reads he was near the pontiff as one of the guards and was struck by some of the bullets aimed at the pontiff. He has need of our fervent prayers now.

The world will never be told of the attempted masquerade. Very few of us know the truth. Many still think Pius is recovering from bullet wounds inflicted during the assassination attempt by Maria Penkova.

Domenico stopped reading. Stunned, he let the dismal news sink into his tired brain. Luciano, dead? Pius back in power? He, the means of protecting Pius? Maria Penkova killed Luciano then had a baby she named Luciana? His hands shook as he continued in stunned disbelief.

> So you see, Domenico, we each had a part to play. *It is my belief that nothing was accidental. Your treachery brought about a good, much like that traitor of old helped to bring about the salvation of the world. Even as it says in the Book, "But we speak of the wisdom of God in a mystery, even the hidden wisdom, which God ordained before the world unto our glory: which none of the princes of this world knew: for had they known it, they would not have crucified the Lord of glory."*[1]

> *I have been authorized to tell you that a date will be set for your ecclesiastical trial in a few days. May the Lord show His mercy to you. Be assured of my prayers.*

> *Yours in Christ,*
> *Carlo Maestoso*

Domenico could have broken out in a fit of hysterical laughter at the bizarre details of all that happened. What he had deemed as a way to usher in a whole new age of liberality for the church had not only failed, but left him totally without any influence or power and in fact under house arrest. All his careful meticulous planning had accomplished nothing. How could he have been so deceived?

Instead of laughter, his throat closed as if he was being choked, and his eyes filled with wetness. Could it all indeed be as Maestoso says? Had he so misjudged God's plan, yet been an active part in it nonetheless? Had the purpose of his life all boiled down to this one failed scheme?

His own father's sad-funny face suddenly popped into his consciousness. Had his "jolly" play acting father been right after all? His father, who had the gift of taking life as it came; who laughed when he felt like laughing, and cried when he felt like crying, was that really the way life should be? Had he misjudged his own father as well? Had his life really been so misguided? Had his life truly been for naught?

---

[1] 1 Corinthians 2:7-8

For the first time in many years, Domenico degli Alfieri felt the oozing of warm moisture on his cheeks. One after the other, the droplets fell onto the letter he had dropped in his lap. He started gagging and broke into a fit of sobbing. He remembered the way his father used to pick him up and dance around the room with him, a happy smile on his face.

"Papa," he had cried in joy then.

"Papa," he cried in anguish now.

The room was soon filled with the sad sound of his wailing.

End

The Main Characters

Domenico delgli Alfieri- Vatican Secretary of State
Carlo Maestoso- a Priest at the Vatican
Maria Penkova – a young, sexy, mentally deranged Bulgarian woman
Pope Pius XIII
Dr. Lucreto-The Pope's physician
Luciano Steidler- A Swiss Guard at the Vatican
Eugeny Gregorovich Basarian- A Soviet Union person
Luis Ramon Conde-del Restrepo- A Latin America person
Alfredo Gianfredo- The Papal Valet
Sister Anna –The assistant cook at the Vatican
Sister Simione – The head cook at the Vatican
Fr. Vittorio Santo, S.J. –The Confessor to the Pope
Wilhwem Franken- Fr. Santo's Brother in Law
Martha- Fr. Santo's Sister
Anna – Fr. Santo's former lover
Il Turco- A sinister underworld person
Antonio- A chef under whom Carlo worked in his father's restaurant
Pietro Campanello- A regular patron of the restaurant
Signore Carozza – The Orient Express Co. Director
Farid el-Khwarizmi- An assistant Chef to Carlo on the Orient Express train
Carmelina- A madam on the Orient Express train
Padre Paolo-A Priest in Venice, Italy
Blago Penkov- Maria Penkova's father
Sophia – Maria Penkova's sister
Sasho – Maria Penkova's classmate
Captain Rocco Baldossari- An Italian Police Officer

The Plot

The liberal Vatican Secretary of State plots to kidnap the current conservative Pope. He intends to replace him with a look-alike person who will lead the Catholic Church in a more liberal direction.

CPSIA information can be obtained at www.ICGtesting.com
Printed in the USA
BVOW09s1610160115

383300BV00005B/117/P

9 781498 417778